ONE EQUALS ZERO

and Other Mathematical Surprises

Paradoxes, Fallacies, and Mind Bogglers

Nitsa Movshovitz-Hadar and John Webb

KEY CURRICULUM PRESS

Innovators in Mathematics Education

Editor: Greer Lleuad
Additional Editorial Development: Sarah Block, Eberhard Scheiffele
Editorial Assistant: Romy Snyder
Copyeditor: Nick Murray
Production Editor: Eleanor Renner Brown
Managing Production Editor: Deborah Cogan
Production Manager: Steve Rogers
Production Coordinator: Diana Krevsky
Cover and Interior Design: Irene Imfeld
Illustrations: Beatrice Benjamin
Technical Illustrations: Irene Imfeld, Jan Camp
Layout: Bruce Saltzman, Digital Type and Image

Editorial Director: John Bergez
Publisher: Steve Rasmussen

Key Curriculum Press
1150 65th Street
Emeryville, CA 94608
510-595-7000
editorial@keypress.com
http://www.keypress.com

Printed in the United States of America.

10 9 8 7 6 5 4 3 2   01 00 99 98

ISBN 1-55953-309-9

This book is dedicated to our families:

Nitsa's—husband Mordechai, and children Tomer, Yoram, Peleg, and Nurit

John's—wife Anthea, and children Ian, Lindy, and Jonathan

The bush burned with fire,
and the bush was not consumed.
Exodus 3.2

Contents

Introduction   vii
Key Concepts Matrix   xi
Recommended Reading   xiii

Activities

1 One Equals Zero   1
2 Four Equals Five   3
3 Every Positive Number Is Greater Than Itself   6
4 A Lucky Mistake   8
5 A Quadratic Equation with Three Roots   10
6 Troubles with the Index Laws   12
7 A Solution That Does Not Check Out   14
8 Another Solution That Does Not Check Out   18
9 Yet Another Solution That Does Not Check Out   20
10 The Lost Solution   23
11 Another Lost Solution   25
12 The Wrong Solution   27
13 2 > 3 by Logarithms   29
14 A Question of Quadratics   31
15 A Fault in the Fractions   33
16 The Largest Prime   36
17 The Bedouin Will   40
18 Discount and Sales Tax   44
19 All Men Are Bald   46
20 The Harder Problem Is Easier to Prove   49
21 The Rising Moon Paradox   52
22 The Rowboat Paradox   56
23 The Angles of a Triangle   58
24 Walking Around a Triangle   63
25 Congruency Paradox   65
26 Every Trapezoid Is a Parallelogram   70
27 Every Triangle Is Isosceles   72
28 All Obtuse Angles Are Right Angles   76

CONTENTS

29	Two Perpendiculars?	80
30	The Empty Circle	83
31	A Two-Piece Jigsaw	86
32	The Surface Area of a Sphere	89
33	The Lost Square	91
34	Earth Versus a Ping-Pong™ Ball	95
35	A Tangram Paradox	97
36	The Ratio of Surface Area to Volume	101
37	Pick's Paradox	103
38	Which Strip Has the Greatest Area?	109
39	The Average Math Score Paradox	113
40	Whose Average?	116
41	Increasing the Average	119
42	Almost Everybody Is Above Average	121
43	Half the World Is Stupid?	123
44	A Chess Tournament Paradox	125
45	The Dice Paradox	129
46	The Random Chord Paradox	132
47	The Tennis Ball Paradox	137
48	Center of Gravity Paradox	139
49	The Paradox of the Locked Boxes	141
50	The Running Dog	143
51	The Explorer Paradox	145
52	A Surprise Limit	147
53	The Quadratic Formula Revisited	149
54	A Stairway to Paradox	151
55	A Calculus Proof That $1 = 2$	154
56	Two Wrongs Make a Right	156
57	Area, Surface, and Volume	158
58	The Alpenhorn Paradox	161
59	The Surprise Test Paradox	164
60	A Surprise Limit Revisited	166

Introduction

How quaint the ways of Paradox!
At common sense she gaily mocks!
W. S. Gilbert

This book is a collection of paradoxes, fallacies, and brain teasers suitable for use in the high school mathematics curriculum. Each of the activities in this book will encourage students to look at familiar mathematical concepts in a new light and deepen their understanding of those concepts.

A paradox is the mathematician's finest joke. A good paradox develops easily, plausibly, and apparently logically until it reaches a punch line that is entirely unbelievable, gaily mocking at common sense. A good paradox, like a good joke, needs to be well told and will provoke anything from an explosive guffaw to a wry smile, followed by a furrowed brow.

As Martin Gardner has observed, paradoxes are also like conjuring tricks. The conjurer, after showing the audience an empty top hat, waves a magic wand and pulls a rabbit out of the hat. How was the trick performed? Where did the rabbit come from? How is it possible that a simple chain of reasoning can lead to the conclusion that one equals zero?

But mathematics is not like magic: conjurers never explain their tricks, yet mathematicians try to explain everything down to the last detail.

Some paradoxes are easily explained because they rely on a simple misuse of a fundamental rule. Perhaps these simple fallacies are not worthy of being called paradoxes at all, merely false arguments. Nevertheless, discussion of simple fallacies goes to the very heart of mathematics: one false assumption may render an entire argument fallacious. The story is told that English mathematician Bertrand Russell (1872–1970) asserted at dinner that a false statement can be used to prove anything. His dinner-table companion challenged him:

"Well, Russell, if I allow you the premise that one is equal to two, can you prove that I am the pope?"

Russell thought for a moment and replied:

"You and the pope are two people. But one is equal to two, so you and the pope are one person. Therefore, you are the pope."

Other paradoxes rely on the fact that the popular use of terms such as *average* or *probability* is sometimes at variance with their strict mathematical definitions. Here we are at the central problem of applied mathematics: fitting our mathematical structures to real-life situations.

Still other paradoxes are very deep and illustrate that the essence of a really good paradox is that no one explanation is ever entirely satisfactory. For example, paradoxes of infinity are especially difficult to unravel, perhaps because the concept of infinity is completely abstract and outside our real-world experience. The great paradoxes of antiquity, such as the paradox of Achilles and the tortoise, were paradoxes of infinity.

Paradoxes are fun but must also be taken seriously, for through the ages paradoxes have been a strong force driving mathematicians to think seriously about the foundations of their subject. The common-sense philosophy of the Pythagoreans that all of mathematics could be encompassed within a theory of whole numbers was mocked by the discovery that the square root of two is not a whole number and cannot be expressed as a quotient of two whole numbers. In relatively recent times the development of calculus was influenced by Irish philosopher Bishop George Berkeley (1685–1753) mercilessly attacking English mathematician Isaac Newton (1642–1727) and German mathematician Gottfried Leibniz (1646–1716) with his paradoxes of infinitesimals. And later, the attempt made by German mathematician Gottlob Frege (1848–1925) to base mathematics on set theory was destroyed by Russell's paradox of the set of all sets that are not members of themselves.

Mathematics is full of paradoxes and can never be free of them. That, paradoxically enough, can be rigorously proved. In the 1930s Austrian logician Kurt Gödel (1906–1978) proved that in any mathematical system that includes ordinary arithmetic there are statements that are undecidable: they make perfect sense but can be neither proved nor disproved. Gödel's theorem proved that the mathematician's work can never be finished. That is the ultimate paradox.

Using this book

A paradox used as a teaching device exploits the idea of cognitive conflict. When you are presenting the paradoxes in this book to students, we suggest that you remain silent and refrain from intervening in order to allow students the space to struggle with the cognitive conflict on their own. Don't deprive students of the pleasure of resolving a conflict themselves. A risk in using cognitive conflict as a teaching technique is that some students may feel confused, frustrated, or deceived. Try to be sensitive to the frustrations of those students who are losing hope and need a hint.

All the one- and two-page activities in this book are student-directed and can be used in algebra, geometry, trigonometry, statistics, or calculus classes. The activities can be used to reinforce, refine, or clarify a concept your students are studying, to add an element of surprise to your mathematics class, to stimulate problem-solving skills, and as discussion topics and extra-credit assignments. Most of the activities can be completed in less than one class period and require no additional materials, although several of the book's geometry activities can be enhanced by the use of geometry computer programs such as The Geometer's Sketchpad®.

Each activity is accompanied by detailed teacher's notes. The explanations in the teacher's notes are limited to the activity and are meant to be shared with students. The comments for each activity are meant for you, the teacher, and are mainly pedagogical and mathematical. For many activities, related historical material follows the comments. Extensions to the activities are often included in this historical material as well as in the comments. Also included in each set of teacher's notes is a list of the activity's key concepts. A matrix of these concepts at the beginning of the book allows you to easily place each activity in a suitable context. Additionally, a list of recommended reading at the beginning of the book guides you and your students to a wealth of related material.

Acknowledgments

The activities in this book were collected over many years of teaching math and have been used in popular lectures for high school students and in more formal seminars for postgraduate students. Thanks are due to many students and colleagues, math teachers, math educators, and mathematicians for many of the ideas for activities we have included in this book.

Although most of the work on this book was completed via the magic of electronic communication, we would like to express our gratitude to the Technion-Israel Institute of Technology, the Israel Ministry of Science, the University of Cape Town, and the South African Foundation for Research Development for supporting our visits to each other so that we could write earlier drafts while on the same continent.

Finally, this book would not have been published without the hand kindly offered to us by Steve Rasmussen, president of Key Curriculum Press, and the energetic and professional work of our editor, Greer Lleuad, who, together with the Key Curriculum staff, brought the manuscript to its present form.

Nitsa Movshovitz-Hadar and John Webb

Key Concepts Matrix

CONCEPT	ACTIVITY	CONCEPT	ACTIVITY
Angle bisectors	27	Equations	1, 2, 5, 8, 9, 15, 54
Angles	28		
Angles, circumferential	27	Equations, cubic	7
Angles inscribed in a semicircle	29	Equations, logarithmic	10, 12
		Equations, quadratic	2, 4, 5, 7, 14, 53
Area	57		
Area between parallel lines	38	Equations, trigonometric	11
Area equivalence	33, 35, 38	Equators	34
Area and perimeter of circles	32	Exponents	54
Area of parallelograms	38	Exponents, multiplication of	6
Area of polygons	37	Exterior points	30
Area of rectangles	38	Fair games	45
Area of triangles	32	Fibonacci sequence	33
Arithmetic-mean –geometric-mean theorem	30	Finite integrals	58
Averages	39, 40, 41, 42, 43	Finite versus infinite probability space	59
		Fractions	17, 39
Binomial formula	9	Fractions, algebraic	15
Canceling zero	1, 7, 15	Functions, logarithmic	13
Cavalieri's principle	38	Functions, trigonometric	60
Chords	46	Geometric decomposition	35
Circles	21, 30, 34, 46	Geometry	22, 52, 60
Circumference	34, 57	Geometry, coordinate	37
Commutative law	18	Geometry, spherical	24
Composite numbers	16	Geometry, three-dimensional	31
Computers in mathematics	16		
Continuity and discontinuity	48	Golden ratio	25
Cubic roots	9	Identities	2, 5
Definitions	19	Identities, trigonometric	11
Derivatives	53, 55, 56, 57, 60	Index laws	2, 6
		Inequalities	3, 13, 20, 39
Distorting theorems	25, 36	Infinite series	47
Dividing by zero	1, 3, 14, 26	Infinite sets	16

KEY CONCEPTS MATRIX

CONCEPT	ACTIVITY	CONCEPT	ACTIVITY
Infinity	47, 49, 50, 51, 58	Pythagorean theorem	30
		Quadrilaterals	26
Interior points	30	Quantifiers, existential and universal	5
Intuition	22, 47	Random choices	46
L'Hospital's rule	53, 60	Rationalizing the denominator	8
Limits	32, 47, 48, 49, 51, 52, 60	Rectangles	28
Logarithms	12	Relying on figures	21, 27, 28, 30, 33, 35, 37
Lucky mistakes	4, 56		
Magic squares	44	Right-angle triangle trigonometry	33
Mathematical induction	19, 20	Roots	6
Mean and median	43	Solids of revolution	58
Midpoints	48	Solutions, existence of	54
Minima and maxima	36	Solutions, extraneous	2, 7, 9, 12
Nonreversible steps	7, 8, 9, 10	Solutions, lost	7, 10, 11, 12
Open sentences	19	Spheres	32, 34
Operations, binary	6	Spheres, surface area of	32
Operations, order of	54	Spheres, volume of	32
Order relations	44, 45	Square roots	2, 54
Parallelograms	26	Surface area and volume of solids	36, 57
Parallel postulate (Euclid's fifth axiom)	23, 24	Surface-area-to-volume ratio	36
Percentages	18	Transitivity	44, 45
Perpendicular bisectors	27	Trapezoids	26
Perpendicular lines	29	Triangle congruency	25
Point of intersection of medians	48	Triangle inequality	25
Polygons	37	Triangle similarity	25, 26
Polyhedra	31	Triangle, sum of the angles of a	23, 24
Prime numbers	16	Triangles, congruent	28
Probability	45	Triangles, isosceles	27
Problems with insufficient data	50	Volume	38
Proofs	27, 28, 34	Word problems	18, 22
Proofs, existence	16	Zero probability	59
Proofs, indirect	20	Zero product	4
Proportional segments	26		
Proportional sharing	17		

Recommended Reading

Abbreviations: Mathematical Association of America (MAA), National Council of Teachers of Mathematics (NCTM)

Allen, R. "Prove a Theorem Using The Geometer's Sketchpad®." *Consortium: The Newsletter of the Consortium for Mathematics and Its Applications* 46 (Summer 1993): 10–11.

Austin, K. "A Paradox: Four Weighings Suffice." *The Mathematical Gazette* 72, no. 460 (1988): 113.

Avital, S., and R. T. Hansen. "Mathematical Induction in the Classroom." *Educational Studies in Mathematics* 7 (1976): 399–411.

Banchoff, T. F. *On the Shoulders of Giants*, Chapter 2. Edited by Arthur Lynn Steen. Washington, DC: National Academy Press, 1990.

Barbeau, E., ed. "Fallacies, Flaws, and Flimflams." *College Mathematics Journal* 20 (January 1989).

Barnette, D. "Map Coloring, Polyhedra, and the Four-Color Problem." In *Dolciani Mathematical Expositions* 8 (1983).

Beiler, A. H. *Recreations in the Theory of Numbers: The Queen of Mathematics Entertains*. Mineola, NY: Dover, 1964.

Borwein J. M. and P. B. "Ramanujan and Pi." *Scientific American* 258, no. 2 (1988): 112–117.

———, and D. H. Baily. "Ramanujan, Modular Equations, and Approximations of Pi, or How to Compute One Billion Digits of Pi." *American Mathematical Monthly* (March 1989).

Boyd, A. V., and M. J. Glencross. "Dissecting a Circle by Chords Through *n* Points." *Mathematics Teacher* (April 1991): 318–319.

Bradis, V. M., V. L. Minkovskii, and A. K. Kharcheve. *Lapses in Mathematical Reasoning*. New York: Pergamon Press, 1963.

Brams, S. *Paradoxes in Politics*. New York: Free Press, 1976.

Brousseau, G., and M. Otte. "The Fragility of Knowledge." In *Mathematical Knowledge: Its Growth Through Teaching*. Edited by A. J. Bishop, S. Mellin-Olsen, and J. van Dormolen. Dodrecht. Vol. 10 of Mathematics Education Library. The Netherlands: Kluwer Academic Publishers Group, 1991.

Bunch, B. H. *Mathematical Fallacies and Paradoxes*. New York: D. Van Nostrand, 1982.

Burke, M. *5-Con Triangles*. (NCTM *Student Math Notes*) (January 1990).

Cajori, F. "Indivisibles and Ghosts of Departed Quantities." *Scientia* 37 (1925): 301–306.

Collingwood, S. D. *The Unknown Lewis Carroll: Eight Major Works and Many Minor*. Mineola, NY: Dover, 1961.

Courant, R., and H. Robins. *What Is Mathematics?* New York: University of Oxford Press, 1948.

Coxeter, H. S. M., et al., eds. *M. C. Escher: Art and Science.* New York: Elsevier Science Publishers B. V., 1986.

Crouse, R. J., and C. W. S. Sloyer. *Mathematical Questions from the Classroom*. Dedham, MA: Janson Publications, 1987.

Dauben, J. W. *G. Cantor: His Mathematics and Philosophy of the Infinite*. Cambridge, MA: Harvard University Press, 1979.

Davis, P. J. "Are There Coincidences in Mathematics?" *American Mathematical Monthly* 88 (1981): 311–320.

———. "Mathematics by Fiat?" *The Two Year College Mathematics Journal* (June 1980): 255–263.

De Morgan, A. *A Budget of Paradoxes*. Edited by D. E. Smith. Chicago: Open Court Publishing, 1915.

Dijkstra, W. E., ed. *Formal Development of Programs and Proofs*. Menlo Park, CA: Addison-Wesley, 1990.

Dubinsky, E. "Teaching Mathematical Induction I." *Journal of Mathematical Behavior* 5 (1986): 305–317.

———. "Teaching Mathematical Induction II." *Journal of Mathematical Behavior* 8 (1990): 285–304.

RECOMMENDED READING

Dubnov, Y. S. *Mistakes in Geometric Proofs.* Boston: D. C. Heath, 1963.

Dunham, W. *Journey Through Genius: The Great Theorems of Mathematics.* New York: John Wiley, 1990.

Dutka, J. "On the St. Petersburg Paradox." *Archives for History of Exact Sciences* 39 (1988): 13–39.

Edwards, C. H. *The Historical Development of the Calculus.* New York: Springer-Verlag, 1979.

Ernest, P. "Mathematical Induction: A Pedagogical Discussion." *Educational Studies in Mathematics* 15 (1984): 173–179.

Eves, H. *Great Moments in Mathematics After 1650.* Washington, DC: MAA, 1982.

——. *Great Moments in Mathematics Before 1650.* Washington, DC: MAA, 1982.

——, and C. V. Newsom. *An Introduction to the Foundations and Fundamental Concepts of Mathematics.* New York: Holt, Rinehart and Winston, 1958.

Fendel, D., and D. Resek. *Exploration and Proof.* Menlo Park, CA: Addison-Wesley, 1990.

Fischbein, E., and I. Engel. "Psychological Difficulties in Understanding the Principle of Mathematical Induction." *Proceedings of the Thirteenth International Conference for the Psychology of Mathematics Education.* Paris, 1989.

Flegg, G. *Paradoxes of the Infinite.* London: Open University Press, 1975.

Fraenkel, A. A. "On the Crisis of the Principle of the Excluded Middle." *Scripta Mathematica* 17 (1951): 5–16.

Gardiner, A. *Infinite Processes: Background to Analysis.* New York: Springer-Verlag, 1982.

Gardner, M. *Aha! Gotcha: Paradoxes to Puzzle and Delight.* New York: W. H. Freeman, 1982.

——. *Hexaflexagons and Other Mathematical Diversions.* Chicago: University of Chicago Press, 1988.

——. *Wheels, Life, and Other Mathematical Amusements.* New York: W. H. Freeman, 1983.

Grattann-Guinness, I., ed. *From the Calculus to Set Theory, 1630–1910: An Introductory History.* London: Duckworth, 1980.

Hacking, I. *The Emergence of Probability.* New York: Cambridge University Press, 1975.

Hadar, N. "An Intuitive Approach to the Logic of Implication." *Educational Studies in Mathematics* 8 (1977): 413–438.

——, and R. Hadass. "Between Associativity and Commutativity." *International Journal of Mathematics Education in Science and Technology* 12, no. 5 (1981): 535–539.

——, and L. Henkin. "Towards a Reliable Test of Conditional Reasoning Ability." *Educational Studies in Mathematics* 9 (1978): 97–114.

Hanna, G. "Proofs That Prove and Proofs That Explain." In Vol. 2 of *Proceedings of the Thirteenth International Conference for the Psychology of Mathematics Education.* Paris, 1989.

Henkin, L. *Mathematical Induction.* MAA Film Manual no. 1. Washington, DC: MAA, 1961.

——. "On Mathematical Induction." *American Mathematical Monthly* 67, no. 4 (1960): 323–338.

Hoffman, P. *Archimedes' Revenge: The Challenge of the Unknown.* New York: W. W. Norton, 1988.

Hofstadter, D. R. *Gödel, Escher, Bach: An Eternal Golden Braid.* New York: Penguin Books, 1979.

Hollingdale, S. *Makers of Mathematics.* London: Pelican Books, 1989.

Honsberger, R. "Mathematical Gems I and II." *Dolciani Mathematical Expositions,* nos. 1 and 2 (1976).

Huck, S. W., and H. M. Sandler. *Statistical Illusions.* New York: Harper and Row, 1984.

Huff, D. *How to Lie With Statistics.* New York: W. W. Norton, 1982.

Jacobs, H. R. *Mathematics: A Human Endeavor: A Textbook for Those Who Think They Don't Like the Subject,* Chapter 10. San Francisco: W. H. Freeman, 1982.

Jargocki, C. P. *Science Brain Twisters, Paradoxes, and Fallacies.* New York: Charles Scribner's, 1976.

Kanigel, R. *The Man Who Knew Infinity: A Life of the Genius Ramanujan.* New York: Macmillan, 1991.

King, J. *Geometry Through the Circle with The Geometer's Sketchpad®.* Berkeley, CA: Key Curriculum Press, 1996.

Kleiner, I. "Thinking the Unthinkable: The Story of Complex Numbers (with a Moral)." *Mathematics Teacher* (October 1988): 583–592.

——, and N. Movshovitz-Hadar. "The Role of Paradoxes in the Evolution of Mathematics." *American Mathematical Monthly* 101, no. 10 (December 1994): 963–974.

Kline, M. *Mathematics: The Loss of Certainty.* New York: Oxford University Press, 1980.

Knuth, D. E. *The Art of Computer Programming*. Vol. 1 of *Fundamental Algorithms*. Menlo Park, CA: Addison-Wesley, 1986.

Kuperman, A. "A Few Comments on Mathematical Induction Mysteries" (in Hebrew). Haifa, Israel: Technion–Israel Institute of Technology, 1990.

Lakatos, I. *Proofs and Refutations: The Logic of Mathematical Discovery*. New York: Cambridge University Press, 1976.

Lénárt, I. *Non-Euclidean Adventures on the Lénárt Sphere*. Berkeley, CA: Key Curriculum Press, 1996.

Linderholm, C. *Mathematics Made Difficult*. London: Wolfe Publishing, 1971.

Lockwood, E. H. *A Book of Curves*. New York: Cambridge University Press, 1961.

Love, W. "Supersolids: Solids Having Finite Volume and Infinite Surface." *Mathematics Teacher* 83, no. 1 (1989): 60–65.

Lowenthal, F., and T. Eisenberg. "Mathematical Induction in School: An Illusion of Rigor." *School Science and Mathematics* 92, no. 5 (1992): 233–238.

Mackie, J. L. *Truth, Probability and Paradoxes*. New York: Oxford University Press, 1973.

Mandelbrot, B. B. *The Fractal Geometry of Nature*. New York: W. H. Freeman, 1983.

Maor, E. *To Infinity and Beyond: A Cultural History of the Infinite*. Boston: Birkhauser Boston, 1987.

The Mathematical Sciences Education Board. *Reshaping School Mathematics: A Philosophy and Framework for Curriculum*. Washington, DC: National Academy Press, 1990.

Mathematics in the Modern World: Readings from "Scientific American." San Francisco: W. H. Freeman, 1968.

Maxwell, E. A. *Fallacies in Mathematics*. New York: Cambridge University Press, 1959.

Middleton, K. P. "The Role of Russell's Paradox in the Development of Twentieth-Century Mathematics." *Pi Mu Epsilon Journal* 8, no. 4 (1986): 234–241. Reviewed in *College Mathematics Journal* 18, no. 1 (January 1987): 80.

Moore, G. H. *Zermello's Axiom of Choice: Its Origins, Development, and Influences*. New York: Springer-Verlag, 1982.

Movshovitz-Hadar, N. "Behold! Polynomial Equations and Their Maximum Number of Real Roots." *Mathematics Teaching* 134 (March 1991): 43.

———. "The False Coin Problem: Mathematical Induction and Knowledge Fragility." *Journal of Mathematical Behavior* 12, no. 3 (1993): 253–268.

———. "The Falsifiability Criterion and Refutation by Mathematical Induction." In Vol. 3 of *Proceedings of the Fifteenth International Conference for the Psychology of Mathematics Education*. Assisi, Italy, 1991.

———. "Mathematical Induction: A Focus on the Conceptual Framework." *School Science and Mathematics* 93, no. 8 (1993): 408–417.

———. "School Mathematics Theorems: An Endless Source of Surprise." *For The Learning of Mathematics: An International Journal of Mathematics Education* 8, no. 3 (1988): 34–40.

———, and N. Daher. "If . . . , then . . . Statements Revisited." In *Proceedings of the Tenth International Conference for the Psychology of Mathematics Education*. London, 1986.

———, and R. Hadass. "More About Mathematical Paradoxes." *Teaching and Teacher Education* 70, no. 1 (1991): 79–92.

———, and R. Hadass. "Preservice Education of Math Teachers Using Paradoxes." *Educational Studies in Mathematics* 21 (1990): 265–287.

———, S. Inbar, and O. Zaslavsky. "Sometimes Students' Errors Are Our Fault." *Educamus* 38, no. 2 (1992): 25–27. Originally published in *Mathematics Teacher* 80, no. 3 (March 1987): 191–194.

———, S. Inbar, and O. Zaslavsky. "Students' Distortions of Theorems." *FOCUS on Learning Problems in Mathematics* 8, no. 1 (1986): 49–57.

———, and A. Shmukler. "A Qualitative Study of Polynomials in High School." *International Journal of Mathematics Education in Science and Technology* 22, no. 4 (1991): 523–543.

———, A. Shmukler, and O. Zaslavsky. "Facilitating an Intuitive Basis for the Fundamental Theorem of Algebra Through Graphical Technologies." *Computers in Mathematics and Science Teaching* 13, no. 3 (1994): 339–364.

Nagel, E., and J. R. Newman. *Gödel's Proof*. New York: New York University Press, 1958.

Niven, I. "A Simple Proof That π Is Irrational." *American Mathematical Monthly: The Bulletin of the American Mathematical Society* 53 (1947): 509.

Northrop, E. P. *Riddles in Mathematics: A Book of Paradoxes*. New York: Robert Kreiger Publishing, 1975.

RECOMMENDED READING

O'Brien, T. C. "Logical Thinking in College Students." *Educational Studies in Mathematics* 5 (1973): 71–79.

Peitgen, H. O., H. Jürgens, and D. Saupe. *Fractals for the Classroom.* New York: Springer-Verlag, 1992.

Peterson, I. *The Mathematical Tourist: Snapshots of Modern Mathematics,* Chapter 5. New York: W. H. Freeman, 1988.

Pólya, G. *Mathematics and Plausible Reasoning.* Vol. 1 of *Induction and Analogy in Mathematics.* Princeton, NJ: Princeton University Press, 1954.

Popper, K. R. *The Logic of Scientific Discovery.* New York: Science Editions, 1961. Translated by the author. Originally published in Vienna, 1934.

Quine, W. *The Ways of Paradoxes and Other Essays.* Cambridge, MA: Harvard University Press, 1976.

Radermacher, H., and O. Toeplitz. *The Enjoyment of Mathematics.* Princeton, NJ: Princeton University Press, 1957.

Ramsamujh, T. I. "A Paradox: All Positive Integers Are Equal." *The Mathematical Gazette* 72, no. 460 (1988): 113.

Reid, W. "Fitting Three Polygons." *PLUS,* no. 17 (Spring 1991): 6–7.

Renyi, A. *Dialogues on Mathematics.* San Francisco: Holden-Day Publishing, 1967.

Rising, G. R., J. H. Graham, J. G. Balzano, J. M. Burt, and A. M. King. *Unified Mathematics Book 3.* Boston: Houghton Mifflin, 1985.

Ross, K. A. *Elementary Analysis.* New York: Springer-Verlag, 1990.

Rucker, R. *Infinity and the Mind.* New York: Bantam Books, 1982.

Russell, B. "Mathematics and the Metaphysicians." *In Mysticism and Logic.* New York: W. W. Norton, 1929.

Schattschneider, D. *M. C. Escher: Visions of Symmetry.* New York: W. H. Freeman, 1990.

Schoenfeld, A., J. Smith, and A. Arcavi. "Learning: The Microgenetic Analysis of One Student's Evolving Understanding of a Complex Subject-Matter Domain." *Advances in Instructional Psychology* 4 (1993): 55–175.

Schroeder, M. *Fractals, Chaos, Power Laws: Minutes for Infinite Paradise.* New York: W. H. Freeman, 1991.

Smullyan, R. *What Is the Name of This Book?* New York: Penguin Books, 1978.

Stewart, I. *Game, Set, and Math: Enigmas and Conundrums.* New York: Penguin Books, 1991.

Struik, D. J. *Mathematics Teacher* 56 (1963): 257–266.

Vinner, S. "Implicit Axioms: w-Rule and the Axiom of Induction in High School Mathematics." *American Mathematical Monthly* 83 (1976): 561–566.

Webb, J. H. "Two Surprising Limits Revisited." *Mathematical Gazette* 67, no. 442 (December 1983): 256–259.

Whitehead, A. N. *The Aims of Education.* New York: Macmillan, 1929.

Wilder, R. L. *The Foundation of Mathematics.* New York: John Wiley, 1965.

Yaglom, A.M. and I. M. *Challenging Mathematical Problems with Elementary Solutions.* New York: Holden-Day Publishing, 1964.

Yaglom, I. M., and V. G. Boltyanskii. *Convex Figures.* Translated by P. J. Kelly and L. F. Walton. New York: Holt, Rinehart, and Winston, 1961.

Zaslavsky, O. "The Development of a Concept: A Trace From the Teacher's Knowledge to a Student's Knowledge." Paper presented at the annual meeting of the AERA, San Francisco, CA, 1989.

1 One Equals Zero

Suppose $x = 1$.

Then
$$x^2 = x$$

$\Rightarrow$
$$x^2 - 1 = x - 1$$

$\Rightarrow$
$$(x - 1)(x + 1) = x - 1$$

$\Rightarrow$
$$(x + 1) = 1$$

$\Rightarrow$
$$x = 0.$$

So $1 = 0$.

Is this possible? What led to this ridiculous conclusion?

1

One Equals Zero

Explanation

The error occurred when the factor $x - 1$ was canceled. Because $x = 1$, $x - 1 = 0$, and it is obviously incorrect to deduce from the statement $0 \cdot (x + 1) = 0$ that $x + 1 = 1$. Canceling factors without considering the possibility that a factor could be zero is a common error.

Comments

- Cancellation is division of both sides of an equation by the same nonzero factor. This activity serves as a warning against dividing both sides of an equation by a factor that could be zero. The purpose of this activity is to accentuate the danger of forgetting that cancellation is defined as dividing both sides by a *nonzero* factor.

- When students have completed this activity, they may consider the formal reason for ruling out division by zero of any nonzero number and for ruling out division by zero of zero, which are very different from each other. The reason in both cases is that division by zero cannot be well defined. Division of a nonzero number by zero is undefined because there is no solution to the equation $a \cdot 0 = b$ if b is *not* zero. If b *is* zero, there are infinitely many solutions to $a \cdot 0 = b$ and division by zero cannot be *uniquely* defined, which is the same as saying that it is not well defined.

See Also

See also Activities 2, 3, 7, 15, and 26.

2 Four Equals Five

Carefully read the following:

$$16 - 36 = 25 - 45 \tag{1}$$

$$\Rightarrow \qquad 16 - 36 + \frac{81}{4} = 25 - 45 + \frac{81}{4} \tag{2}$$

$$\Rightarrow \qquad 4^2 - 2 \cdot 4 \cdot \frac{9}{2} + \left(\frac{9}{2}\right)^2 = 5^2 - 2 \cdot 5 \cdot \frac{9}{2} + \left(\frac{9}{2}\right)^2 \tag{3}$$

$$\Rightarrow \qquad \left(4 - \frac{9}{2}\right)^2 = \left(5 - \frac{9}{2}\right)^2 \tag{4}$$

$$\Rightarrow \qquad 4 - \frac{9}{2} = 5 - \frac{9}{2} \tag{5}$$

$$\Rightarrow \qquad 4 = 5. \tag{6}$$

The reasoning used to reach the conclusion that 4 = 5 began with a statement that is obviously true (16 − 36 and 25 − 45 are both equal to −20) and ended with a statement that is obviously false (4 = 5). What went wrong?

KEY CONCEPTS
- Equations
- Equations, quadratic
- Identities
- Solutions, extraneous
- Square roots

2

Four Equals Five

Explanation

All the steps in the reasoning are correct except the step from equation 4 to equation 5:

$$\left(4 - \frac{9}{2}\right)^2 = \left(5 - \frac{9}{2}\right)^2 \Rightarrow 4 - \frac{9}{2} = 5 - \frac{9}{2}.$$

In general $a^2 = b^2 \Rightarrow a = b$ or $a = -b$, as the following algebraic reasoning shows:

$$a^2 = b^2 \Rightarrow a^2 - b^2 = 0 \Rightarrow (a - b)(a + b) = 0$$

$$\Rightarrow a - b = 0 \text{ or } a + b = 0 \Rightarrow a = b \text{ or } a = -b.$$

So by correctly deducing from $\left(4 - \frac{9}{2}\right)^2 = \left(5 - \frac{9}{2}\right)^2$ that *either* $4 - \frac{9}{2} = 5 - \frac{9}{2}$ (false) *or* $4 - \frac{9}{2} = -\left(5 - \frac{9}{2}\right)$ (true), the paradox disappears.

Comments

- It is common for students to write $\sqrt{x^2} = x$, and that is the source of the confusion caused by this paradox. A correct statement is $\sqrt{x^2} = |x|$, which is how the modulus function is sometimes defined.

- The incorrect statement $\sqrt{x^2} = x$ (which is false if x is negative) is often written $(x^2)^{1/2} = x$. Writing the statement in this way is an example of misusing the index laws. It is true that $(a^m)^n = a^{mn}$ for integer values of m and n and for any value of a, both positive and negative. It is also true that $(a^m)^n = a^{mn}$ if a is positive and m and n are real. However, this statement may *not* be true if a is negative and m and n are not integers.

- The square root notation ($\sqrt{}$) gives some difficulty to students. It needs to be stressed that $\sqrt{a}$ is defined as the positive square root of a and is not a two-valued concept. Thus, it is correct to write $\sqrt{9} = 3$ and $-\sqrt{9} = -3$, but it is not correct to write $\sqrt{9} = \pm 3$. (The correct notation is $\pm\sqrt{9} = \pm 3$.)

- The confusion about the square root notation probably originates with the language we use regarding the notation. It is correct to state that 9 has two square roots, +3 and −3, because these are the two solutions to the equation $x^2 = 9$. But although it is incorrect to write $\sqrt{9} = -3$, the notation $\sqrt{9}$ is often read as "the square root of 9" or just "root 9," which students often confuse with stating that −3 is a square root of 9. Similar comments apply to the notation $9^{1/2}$, which means exactly the same thing as $\sqrt{9}$.

- In the same vein, it is interesting that some students will write $\sqrt{9} = \pm 3$ but will regard $\sqrt{2}$ as a positive number, not as a pair of numbers. Additionally, the confusion in students' minds about the meaning of the square root notation is probably reinforced by the term $\pm\sqrt{b^2 - 4ac}$, which occurs in the formula for the solution of the quadratic equation.

- The "proof" that $4 = 5$ can be generalized to "prove" that $x = x + 1$ for all x:

Begin with $x^2 - x(2x + 1) = (x + 1)^2 - (x + 1)(2x + 1)$ (which is true, because both sides are equal to $-x^2 - x$).

Complete the square on both sides by adding $\left[\frac{1}{2}(2x + 1)\right]^2$:

$$x^2 - x(2x + 1) + \left[\frac{1}{2}(2x + 1)\right]^2 = (x + 1)^2 - (x + 1)(2x + 1) + \left[\frac{1}{2}(2x + 1)\right]^2$$

$$\Rightarrow \left[x - \frac{1}{2}(2x + 1)\right]^2 = \left[(x + 1) - \frac{1}{2}(2x + 1)\right]^2$$

$$\Rightarrow \left[x - \frac{1}{2}(2x + 1)\right] = (x + 1) - \frac{1}{2}(2x + 1)$$

$$\Rightarrow \qquad\qquad x = x + 1.$$

In particular, this argument apparently proves that any two consecutive integers are equal!

See Also

For more about index laws, see Activity 6.

3 Every Positive Number Is Greater Than Itself

Each of the proofs below seems to prove that every positive number is greater than itself. How can that be?

Proof 1:

Suppose that $a > 0$, and let $b = \frac{1}{2}a$. Then $a > b > 0$

$$\text{and } ab > b^2.$$
$$\Rightarrow \quad ab - a^2 > b^2 - a^2$$
$$\Rightarrow \quad a(b - a) > (b - a)(b + a)$$
$$\Rightarrow \quad a > b + a$$
$$\Rightarrow \quad a > a.$$

What led to this conclusion?

Proof 2:

Suppose that $a > 0$, and let $b = a$. Then

$$ab = b^2$$
$$\Rightarrow \quad ab - a^2 = b^2 - a^2$$
$$\Rightarrow \quad a(b - a) = (b - a)(b + a)$$
$$\Rightarrow \quad a = b + a$$
$$\Rightarrow \quad a > a.$$

What led to this conclusion?

3

Every Positive Number Is Greater Than Itself

Explanation

The mistake in the first proof is the division of the inequality by the negative number $b - a$ without changing the direction of the inequality. The mistake in the second proof is the cancellation of the factor $b - a$, which is zero.

Comments

- A very common mistake made in treating inequalities is to multiply or divide by a negative number without reversing the inequality sign. The first proof in this activity shows how this error can lead to an absurd conclusion.

- The second proof highlights another very common error that is hard to eliminate: dividing by zero. Paradoxes are a very effective way to convince students of the danger of this error.

Here is another example:

$$\text{Solve for } x: \quad 6x - 10 = 21x - 35.$$

$$\text{"Solution":} \quad 2(3x - 5) = 7(3x - 5).$$

$$\text{Therefore,} \quad 2 = 7.$$

The last step used to solve the equation is incorrect because the possibility that $3x - 5$ is zero has been overlooked. If $3x - 5 = 0$, then $x = \frac{5}{3}$, which is the correct solution of the equation.

See Also

See also the comments in Activity 1.

4   A Lucky Mistake

Henry solved the equation $-x^2 + x + 6 = 4$ as follows:

$$(3 - x)(x + 2) = 4$$

$$x + 2 = 4, \text{ or } 3 - x = 4$$

$$x = 2, \text{ or } x = -1.$$

He checked his solutions by substituting them into the original equation and found that they worked. (See if you can verify his check.)

Next he tackled the equation $-x^2 - 3x + 10 = 6$. He proceeded as follows:

$$(5 + x)(2 - x) = 6$$

$$5 + x = 6, \text{ or } 2 - x = 6$$

$$x = 1, \text{ or } x = -4.$$

Again both solutions checked out.

Then he multiplied the equation by -1 to obtain a more "standard" form, $x^2 + 3x - 10 = -6$. He applied his method again:

$$(x + 5)(x - 2) = -6$$

$$x + 5 = -6, \text{ or } x - 2 = -6$$

$$x = -11, \text{ or } x = -4.$$

But this time the solution $x = -11$ did not check out.

What went wrong?

One Equals Zero and Other Mathematical Surprises ©1998 by Key Curriculum Press

4

A Lucky Mistake

Explanation

Henry's method produced correct answers in the first two cases purely by chance. The correct method for solving a quadratic equation is to resolve it into factors in the form $(x - a)(x - b) = 0$, then deduce that one of the factors is 0. Henry's version of this method amounts to saying that if the product of two numbers is c, then one of the numbers is c, a valid rule only if $c = 0$.

Comments

- Incorrect methods used to produce correct answers by pure chance are difficult for students and teachers to detect. Persuading students to give up incorrect methods can be particularly difficult. A good way to help students see that a method is faulty is to show them examples for which that method fails.

- A well-known lucky mistake is the "cancellation" law by which $\frac{16}{64} = \frac{1}{4}$ as a result of striking out the 6 in the numerator and in the denominator. Applied in another case, this law would result in $\frac{13}{32} = \frac{1}{2}$, which is obviously wrong.

  Another lucky mistake results in the equation $(a - b)(a + b) = a^2 - b^2$, obtained by multiplying a by a and b by $-b$. You can examine whether students used a valid method to work out this equation by asking them to work out $(a + b)(a + b)$. If they get the answer $a^2 + b^2$, they are using the wrong method, of course. (For another lucky mistake, see Activity 56.)

- A worthwhile, quite difficult problem to give students is to find out for which numbers a, b, and c Henry's method of solving $x^2 + bx + c = a$ works.

  It is interesting that quite a large class of equations are solvable by Henry's over-generalization method, namely all equations of the form $(a - x)(x + b) = a + b - 1$. On the other hand, no equation of the form $(x + a)(x + b) = c$, if $c \neq 0$, is correctly solvable by Henry's method.

---

5 A Quadratic Equation with Three Roots

If *a*, *b*, and *c* are different real numbers, then the equation

$$\frac{(x - a)(x - b)}{(c - a)(c - b)} + \frac{(x - b)(x - c)}{(a - b)(a - c)} + \frac{(x - a)(x - c)}{(b - a)(b - c)} = 1$$

is a quadratic equation satisfied by *a*, *b*, and *c*. But a quadratic equation can never have three roots.

What is wrong here?

One Equals Zero and Other Mathematical Surprises ©1998 by Key Curriculum Press

5

A Quadratic Equation with Three Roots

Explanation

The equation appears to be quadratic, but it is not: The coefficient of x^2 is

$$\frac{1}{(c-a)(c-b)} + \frac{1}{(a-b)(a-c)} + \frac{1}{(b-c)(b-a)}$$

$$= \frac{(b-a) + (c-b) + (a-c)}{(a-b)(b-c)(c-a)}$$

$$= 0.$$

A similar calculation shows that the coefficient of x is 0 and that the constant coefficient on the left-hand side of the equation is 1. Thus, the original equation is not really an equation because it reduces to the identity of $1 = 1$.

In its original form, the equation is an identity satisfied by any value of x; a, b, and c are just three of those values.

Comments

- A simpler version of this paradox begins with the equation $\frac{(x-a)}{(b-a)} + \frac{(x-b)}{(a-b)} = 1$ if $a \neq b$.

  The equation appears to be linear but clearly has two solutions: $x = a$ and $x = b$. Here it is easier to see that the coefficient of x is zero and that the equation reduces to the identity $1 = 1$.

- Students often fail to distinguish between an identity and an equation. In an equation the equality is existential: *there exists* an x such that $f(x) = g(x)$ if f and g are expressions in x. In an identity the equality is universal: *for all x*, $f(x) = g(x)$. Usually, students are assigned very different tasks regarding equations and identities. Students are asked to *solve* an equation, that is, to find *all* values of the variable that make the *given* equality a true sentence. Students are asked to *prove* an identity, that is, to demonstrate that the equality actually holds for *every* value.

- This activity will be valuable only for students who already know that a quadratic equation has at most two real solutions, and are able to identify $(x-a)(x-b)$ as a quadratic expression. Otherwise, students will not be surprised by finding more than two solutions.

6 Trouble with the Index Laws

Ahmad and Betsy argued over the value of $(-8)^{1/3}$.

Ahmad said its value was -2 because $(-8)^{1/3}$ means "the cube root of -8" and $(-2)^3 = -8$.

Betsy argued that $(-8)^{1/3} = (-8)^{2/6} = [(-8)^2]^{1/6} = 64^{1/6} = 2$.

Who is correct?

One Equals Zero and Other Mathematical Surprises ©1998 by Key Curriculum Press

6

Trouble with the Index Laws

Explanation

Ahmad's reasoning is correct. Betsy obtained the wrong answer by misusing the index laws. She wrote $(-8)^{2/6} = [(-8^2)]^{1/6}$, applying the index law, $a^{mn} = (a^m)^n$.

However, this index law holds for integer values of m and n and cannot be applied to noninteger values without risk, especially if a is negative.

For example, $[(-2)^2]^{1/2} = 4^{1/2} = 2$, but $(-2)^{(2 \cdot 1/2)} = (-2)^1 = -2$.

Comment

Paradoxical results such as $4 = 5$ can also be obtained if the index law, $\sqrt{x^2} = |x|$, is wrongly applied as $\sqrt{x^2} = x$, which is incorrect if x is negative. (See also Activity 2.)

---

7 A Solution That Does Not Check Out

Mary was asked to solve the equation

$$x - x^2 = 1. \tag{1}$$

She observed that $x = 0$ does not satisfy the equation, so she divided the equation by x: $1 - x = \frac{1}{x}$, or

$$x + \frac{1}{x} = 1. \tag{2}$$

From equations 1 and 2 she deduced the following:

$$x - x^2 = x + \frac{1}{x} \tag{3}$$

$$-x^2 = \frac{1}{x}$$

$$x^3 = -1$$

$$x = -1.$$

But when she substituted −1 into equation 1, she found her solution did not check out.

Can you explain why?

KEY CONCEPTS
- Equations, cubic
- Equations, quadratic
- Nonreversible steps
- Solutions, extraneous
- Solutions, lost

7

A Solution That Does Not Check Out

Explanation

Mary showed that, assuming the original equation had a real solution, it followed that the solution had to be −1. However, −1 turned out not to be a solution. Therefore, the original equation has no real solution.

The false solution resulted from a nonreversible step. Combining equations 1 and 2 to get equation 3 is correct, but deducing equation 1 or equation 2 from equation 3 is not possible.

Comments

- Note that Mary's last step (deducing that $x = -1$ from $x^3 = -1$) involved canceling a zero factor:

$$x^3 = -1$$

$$\Rightarrow \qquad x^3 + 1 = 0$$

$$\Rightarrow \quad (x + 1)(x^2 - x + 1) = 0$$

$$\Rightarrow \qquad x = -1, \text{ or } x^2 - x + 1 = 0$$

(The latter equation in the last step is equivalent to the original equation.)

For more about canceling a zero factor, see Activity 1.

- Introducing false solutions by faulty algebraic manipulation is a very common error. This activity illuminates this error and provides you with an opportunity to focus students' attention on the logic underlying the solution of equations. In particular, the activity demonstrates the risk of applying a nonreversible step when solving an equation.

Let's take a careful look at the logic behind solving an equation. Suppose we start with an equation of the form $f(x) = 0$. Solving this equation involves applying a number of different algebraic operations, such as cross-multiplying, transposing, factoring, and so on. Our goal is to transform the equation to the form $g(x) = 0$, from which solutions can be easily obtained.

For example, the equation $x^3 + 2x^2 - x - 2 = 0$ becomes, after factoring, $(x - 1)(x + 1)(x + 2) = 0$, and the solutions are $x = -1$, $x = 1$, and $x = -2$. Similarly, the trigonometric equation $\cos x + \sin x = 0$ becomes $\sin(x + 45°) = 0$, giving solutions $x = -45° + n180°(n \in Z)$.

During the process of converting the original equation $f(x) = 0$ to the solvable equation $g(x) = 0$, it is important that no solutions are lost and no false solutions are introduced. The process of converting the original equation $f(x) = 0$ to the solvable equation $g(x) = 0$ is usually called the solution process. If at every stage of the solution process the steps of the process are reversible, so that $f(x) = 0 \Leftrightarrow g(x) = 0$, then the solutions read off from $g(x) = 0$ are precisely the same as those satisfying $f(x) = 0$, no more, no less. However, if the manipulations are not reversible, and we have only the one-way implication $f(x) = 0 \Rightarrow g(x) = 0$, then $\{x: f(x) = 0\} \subsetneqq \{x: g(x) = 0\}$ and there are solutions of $g(x) = 0$ that are not solutions of $f(x) = 0$.

Example: Solve for x: $\sqrt{x + 1} - x + 1 = 0$.

$$\sqrt{x + 1} - x + 1 = 0$$

$$\Leftrightarrow \quad \sqrt{x + 1} = x - 1$$

$$\Rightarrow \quad x + 1 = (x - 1)^2$$

$$\Leftrightarrow \quad x^2 - 3x = 0$$

$$\Leftrightarrow \quad x(x - 3) = 0$$

$$\Leftrightarrow \quad x = 0, \text{ or } x = 3.$$

Only $x = 3$ is a solution of the original equation. Note that $\sqrt{x + 1} = x - 1 \Rightarrow x + 1 = (x - 1)^2$ is a nonreversible step—it was here that the false solution was introduced.

Sometimes solutions are lost when an algebraic step is used that is not valid because the logical implication is in the wrong direction.

Example: Solve for x: $\log x^2 = 2 \log 3$.

$$\log x^2 = 2 \log 3$$

$$2 \log x = 2 \log 3$$

$$\log x = \log 3$$

$$x = 3.$$

However, another solution of $\log x^2 = 2 \log 3$ is $x = -3$. How did this solution get lost? Inserting the precise logical connectors between the lines gives

$$\log x^2 = 2 \log 3$$

$$\Leftarrow \quad 2 \log x = 2 \log 3$$

$$\Leftrightarrow \quad \log x = \log 3$$

$$\Leftrightarrow \quad x = 3.$$

The solution $x = -3$ was lost at the second step. A correct manipulation is

$$\log x^2 = 2 \log 3$$

$$\Leftrightarrow \quad 2 \log |x| = 2 \log 3$$

$$\Leftrightarrow \quad \log |x| = \log 3$$

$$\Leftrightarrow \quad x = 3 \text{ or } -3.$$

(For more examples, see Activity 10.)

Summing up, we see that the correct use of the logical connectors $\Rightarrow$, $\Leftarrow$, and $\Leftrightarrow$ indicates whether a solution process is correct or indicates at what point solutions have been lost or false solutions have been introduced. If all the logical connectors in the solution process are $\Leftrightarrow$, the solutions are exactly right. (Note that computational errors can still occur here, which results in solutions that are not exactly right.) If $\Leftarrow$ appears, solutions have been lost. If $\Rightarrow$ appears, extra solutions have been introduced. And if two steps in the solution process are related by neither $\Leftarrow$ nor $\Rightarrow$, the whole solution is suspect. Similarly, if at one step we have $\Leftarrow$ and at another $\Rightarrow$, the whole solution is in doubt. (See also the comments in Activities 4, 8, 9, 10, 11, and 12.)

8 Another Solution That Does Not Check Out

Kim tried to solve the equation

$$\sqrt{x^2 + 16} + \sqrt{x^2 + 7} = 1. \tag{1}$$

He knew that squaring both sides could introduce new solutions, so he tried another approach.

First he inverted both sides of the equation:

$$\frac{1}{\sqrt{x^2 + 16} + \sqrt{x^2 + 7}} = 1.$$

He then rationalized the denominator:

$$\frac{1}{\sqrt{x^2 + 16} + \sqrt{x^2 + 7}} \cdot \frac{\sqrt{x^2 + 16} - \sqrt{x^2 + 7}}{\sqrt{x^2 + 16} - \sqrt{x^2 + 7}} = 1$$

$$\Leftrightarrow \quad \frac{\sqrt{x^2 + 16} - \sqrt{x^2 + 7}}{(x^2 + 16) - (x^2 + 7)} = 1$$

$$\Leftrightarrow \quad \sqrt{x^2 + 16} - \sqrt{x^2 + 7} = 9. \tag{2}$$

Adding equations 1 and 2 gives

$$2\sqrt{x^2 + 16} = 10. \tag{3}$$

$$\Leftrightarrow \quad x^2 + 16 = 25$$

$$\Leftrightarrow \quad x^2 = 9$$

$$\Leftrightarrow \quad x = \pm 3.$$

However, when Kim checked his solutions by substituting them into the original equation, he found that neither solution was valid. Is this right?

What went wrong?

8

Another Solution That Does Not Check Out

Explanation

Kim's manipulation correctly showed that equations 1 and 2 are equivalent. Adding them produced equation 3, which Kim correctly solved. However, deriving equation 3 from equations 1 and 2 is a nonreversible step, and that is where the false solutions were introduced.

Comments

- Kim could have noticed right at the start that equation 1 has no solution because $\sqrt{x^2 + 16} + \sqrt{x^2 + 7} > 1$ for all x.

- Kim could also have noticed that if he had subtracted equation 2 from equation 1 instead of adding equations 1 and 2, he would have obtained $2\sqrt{x^2 + 7} = -8$, which clearly has no solution.

- But Kim did not notice these things, so he implicitly assumed at the outset of the problem that the equation had a solution. When we assume something false, it is not at all surprising when our logic produces a false result.

9 Yet Another Solution That Does Not Check Out

Susan was asked to solve the equation

$$\sqrt[3]{1-x} + \sqrt[3]{x-3} = 1. \qquad (1)$$

She began by cubing both sides, remembering that

$$(a+b)^3 = a^3 + b^3 + 3ab(a+b).$$

This gave

$$(1-x) + (x-3) + 3\left(\sqrt[3]{1-x}\ \sqrt[3]{x-3}\right)\left(\sqrt[3]{1-x} + \sqrt[3]{x-3}\right) = 1. \qquad (2)$$

Susan then substituted the original equation into equation 2, which simplified to

$$3\sqrt[3]{1-x}\ \sqrt[3]{x-3} = 3 \qquad (3)$$

$$(1-x)(x-3) = 1$$

$$-x^2 + 4x - 3 = 1$$

$$x^2 - 4x + 4 = 0$$

$$(x-2)^2 = 0$$

$$x = 2. \qquad (4)$$

However, when Susan substituted $x = 2$ into the original equation, the result was

$$\sqrt[3]{1-2} + \sqrt[3]{2-3} = 1$$

$$(-1) + (-1) = 1.$$

What went wrong?

KEY CONCEPTS
- Binomial formula
- Cubic roots
- Equations
- Nonreversible steps
- Solutions, extraneous

9

Yet Another Solution That Does Not Check Out

Explanation

One simple answer is that nothing went wrong and that there was no error in the reasoning. Susan showed that, assuming equation 1 has a solution, it follows that the solution is $x = 2$. Because $x = 2$ is not a solution, the equation has no solutions.

There remains a technical question: How did the algebraic process in this activity give rise to a spurious solution? At what stage in Susan's reasoning did a false solution creep in? Clearly equations 1 and 2 are equivalent, and the steps from equation 3 to equation 4 are reversible. However, the step from equation 2 to equation 3 cannot be reversed, and that is where the false solution was introduced.

Comments

- Substituting the given equation in the process of solving it, as Susan did in the transition from equation 2 to equation 3, can be a risky step. Doing so implicitly assumes that there exists a value for x that makes the two sides of the equation equal. If indeed there is such a value, the substitution of one side for the other is legitimate in the sense that the solution set remains unchanged. However, when the original equation has no solution, the substitution may be nonreversible and therefore may yield a result that does not check out.

- This activity focuses on the very existence of solutions as the assumption underlying any attempt to solve an equation. An equation is commonly treated as an existential statement. For example, "$x + 3 = 5$" is interpreted as "There exists a value for x such that if 3 is added to it, the sum is 5." The challenge is then to determine that value. But be aware that "Solve for x, $f(x) = 0$" does not necessarily mean there is a solution. Additionally, the transition steps from one equality to another do not presuppose the existence of a solution. These steps are actually conditional statements of the form "If x solves $f(x) = 0$, then x solves $g(x) = 0$." Each of them guarantees that the solution set of $f(x)$ is preserved as a subset of the solution set of $g(x)$. (See also the comments in Activity 7 about the risk of adding or losing a solution in the process of solving an equation.)

- At this point it might be useful to discuss with students the distinction between the logic that underlies solving an equation and the logic that underlies proving an identity. In solving an equation, the equality is *given* and we usually assume there is at least one value that, when substituted for

---

the variable, satisfies the equality. The goal then is to find that value. Proving an identity means establishing it as a universal statement. For example, proving that the equality $a^2 - b^2 = (a + b)(a - b)$ is an identity means proving that it is universally true for all (real) values a and b.

- This activity uses the identity $(a + b)^3 = a^3 + b^3 + 3ab(a + b)$ for cubing a binomial. This formula resembles $(a + b)^2 = a^2 + b^2 + 2ab$, the formula for squaring a binomial, and is worth noting.

10 The Lost Solution

Gilberto solved an equation involving the log function:

$$\log(x - 1)^2 = 2 \log 3$$
$$2 \log(x - 1) = 2 \log 3$$
$$\log(x - 1) = \log 3$$
$$x - 1 = 3$$
$$x = 4.$$

He checked his solution by substituting it into the original equation and found that it worked. However, his friend Reatha pointed out to him that her solution was −2. Was Reatha's solution correct? At what stage in Gilberto's argument did this solution get lost?

10

The Lost Solution

Explanation

Because $\log(-2-1)^2 = \log(-3)^2 = \log 9 = 2 \log 3$, Reatha was quite correct in saying that $x = -2$ is also a solution.

How did Gilberto come to miss Reatha's solution? In his second step he used the rule $\log a^2 = 2 \log a$, which is true for all $a > 0$. For $a < 0$ the rule becomes $\log a^2 = 2 \log|a|$. So when Gilberto changed $\log(x-1)^2$ to $2 \log(x-1)$, he restricted his solution to values of $x > 1$. He would have found the correct solution if he had changed $\log(x-1)^2$ to $2 \log|x-1|$, producing the equation $2 \log|x-1| = 2 \log 3$, which leads to $|x-1| = 3$, giving $x = 4$, or $x = -2$. (See also the comments in Activity 7.)

Comments

- Another approach that does not lose a solution is

$$\log(x-1)^2 = 2 \log 3$$
$$\Leftrightarrow \quad \log(x-1)^2 = \log 3^2$$
$$\Leftrightarrow \quad (x-1)^2 = 9$$
$$\Leftrightarrow \quad x-1 = 3, \text{ or } x-1 = -3$$
$$\Leftrightarrow \quad x = 4, \text{ or } x = -2.$$

- It is not difficult to construct examples of incomplete solution sets that result from a lost solution like that shown in this activity. Here is another one.

Solve for x: $\log(x+1)^2 + \log(x+9)^2 = 2 \log 9$.

This equation has four solutions: $x = 0$, $x = -10$, and $x = -5 \pm \sqrt{7}$. But many students lose two of the answers because they fail to consider the possibility that $x + 1$ and $x + 9$ may not be positive and that hence their absolute values should be considered.

See Also

See also Activities 8, 9, 11, and 12, and the comments in Activities 4 and 7.

11 Another Lost Solution

If you were asked to solve the equation $\tan(x + 45°) = 2 \cot x - 1$, you would probably do something like this:

$$\frac{\tan x + \tan 45°}{1 - \tan 45° \cdot \tan x} = \frac{2}{\tan x} - 1.$$

Substitute $y = \tan x$:

$$\frac{y + 1}{1 - y} = \frac{2}{y} - 1.$$

Solve for y:

$$y = \frac{1}{2}.$$

Therefore, $x = \tan^{-1}\left(\frac{1}{2}\right) + k \cdot 180°$ if k is an integer.

This solution is correct, but there is another infinite set of solutions that was lost on the way to this solution. For example, try substituting 90° into the original equation. Is it a solution? Can you find other solutions that were lost? Why did they disappear?

11

Another Lost Solution

Explanation

In the first step of this activity, two identities were used:

$$\tan(x + 45°) = \frac{\tan x + \tan 45°}{1 - \tan 45° \cdot \tan x} \qquad (1)$$

and

$$\cot x = \frac{1}{\tan x}. \qquad (2)$$

Identity 1 is valid for all x for which $\tan x \neq 1$ (that is, $x \neq 45° + k \cdot 90°$), and identity 2 is valid for all x for which $\tan x \neq 0$ and $\cot x \neq 0$ (that is, $x \neq k \cdot 90°$). None of the first set of values excluded by applying the first identity are solutions to the original equation, but all the values excluded by applying the second identity are solutions. Thus an infinite set of solutions was overlooked by applying the second identity.

Comments

- This activity highlights the care that must be taken in solving equations. Here two identities were used that were not quite identities: they hold for *almost all* values. The use of the first identity did not affect the solution set, but the use of the second identity caused some solutions to be lost.

- To avoid losing solutions, we must make explicit any exclusion of values in the process of solving an equation. These excluded values must be checked separately to examine whether they belong to the solution set or not.

See Also

See also Activities 8, 9, 10, and 12, and the comments in Activities 4 and 7.

   One Equals Zero and Other Mathematical Surprises ©1998 by Key Curriculum Press

12 The Wrong Solution

Kate solved the equation

$$\log[(x + 3)(x - 8)] + \log\left(\frac{x + 3}{x - 8}\right) = 2 \qquad (1)$$

as follows (logarithms are expressed in base 10):

She used the basic log laws first:

$$\log(x + 3) + \log(x - 8) + \log(x + 3) - \log(x - 8) = 2. \qquad (2)$$

She then simplified to

$$2 \log(x + 3) = 2, \qquad (3)$$

giving $x + 3 = 10$, and hence $x = 7$.

However, when she substituted her value into the original equation, she found that neither term on the left-hand side of the equation was defined, so her answer was certainly wrong. Moreover, her friend Jason had used a different method to solve the equation and had found the solution $x = -13$, which worked. What was wrong with Kate's method? Where did the false solution creep in, and where did the correct solution get lost?

12

The Wrong Solution

Explanation

Kate used the basic logarithm laws, $\log AB = \log A + \log B$ and $\log\frac{A}{B} = \log A - \log B$, which are only valid for positive values of A and B. So her first step, from equation 1 to equation 2, was not valid, and that is where she lost the correct solution.

Her next step, from equation 2 to equation 3, was a correct deduction that led to the solution $x = 7$. But although $x = 7$ is a solution of equation 3, it is not a solution of equation 2. To get from equation 3 to equation 2 requires inserting two terms, $\log(x - 8)$ and $-\log(x - 8)$, neither of which is defined when $x = 7$. So the step from equation 2 to equation 3 is not reversible, and that is where Kate introduced the false solution.

Comments

- Kate should have begun solving the equation by assuming that $(x + 3)(x - 8)$ and $\frac{x+3}{x-8}$ are both positive (in fact, if one is positive, so is the other):

$$\log|(x + 3)(x - 8)| + \log\left|\frac{x + 3}{x - 8}\right| = 2$$

$$\Leftrightarrow \quad \log|x + 3| + \log|x - 8| + \log|x + 3| - \log|x - 8| = 2$$

$$\Leftrightarrow \quad 2\log|x + 3| = 2$$

$$\Leftrightarrow \quad \log|x + 3| = 1$$

$$\Leftrightarrow \quad |x + 3| = 10$$

$$\Leftrightarrow \quad x = 7, \text{ or } x = -13.$$

However, because she initially assumed that $(x + 3)(x - 8) > 0$—that is, that $x > 8$ or that $x < -3$—only the solution $x = -13$ was valid.

- This activity emphasizes that if both A and B are negative numbers, then AB is positive and $\log AB$ and $\log \frac{A}{B}$ are both defined. However, neither $\log A$ nor $\log B$ is defined, so the log laws must be written $\log AB = \log|A| + \log|B|$ and $\log \frac{A}{B} = \log|A| - \log|B|$.

  Separately, $\log A$ and $\log B$ have a meaning if $A > 0$ and $B > 0$. Yet $\log AB$ is meaningful if $A > 0$ and $B > 0$ or if $A < 0$ and $B < 0$. (See also Activity 10.)

- You can use this activity to convince students that it is necessary to check whether a result they obtain is within the domain of the definition of the functions involved in the equation. Neglecting this step may lead to "solutions" that actually are not solutions, as happened in this activity.

13 2 > 3 by Logarithms

We know that $\frac{1}{4} > \frac{1}{8}$.

Therefore, $\left(\frac{1}{2}\right)^2 > \left(\frac{1}{2}\right)^3$.

Find the logarithms of both sides of the equation to base a for $a > 0$ and $a \neq 1$. Then,

$$\log_a\left(\frac{1}{2}\right)^2 > \log_a\left(\frac{1}{2}\right)^3,$$

giving

$$2\log_a\left(\frac{1}{2}\right) > 3\log_a\left(\frac{1}{2}\right)$$

or

$$2 > 3.$$

How can that be?

13

2 > 3 by Logarithms

Explanation

The error occurs in one of two places, depending on the value of a. If $a > 1$, then $\log_a\left(\frac{1}{2}\right) < 0$ and the last step in the solution involves dividing the inequality by a negative number. On the other hand, if $0 < a < 1$, then $\log_a\left(\frac{1}{2}\right) > 0$ and the last step is valid. But for $0 < a < 1$, $\log_a x$ is a decreasing function and the third step is wrong: the step should be

$$\left(\frac{1}{2}\right)^2 > \left(\frac{1}{2}\right)^3 \Rightarrow \log_a\left(\frac{1}{2}\right)^2 < \log_a\left(\frac{1}{2}\right)^3.$$

Comments

- This activity can help emphasize the difference between logarithmic functions to different (positive) bases, particularly bases less than 1 and greater than 1.

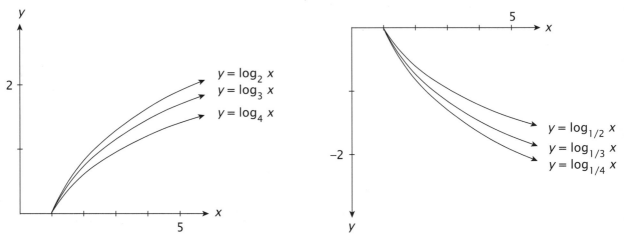

Figure 1: Bases greater than 1   Figure 2: Bases less than 1

- This activity also serves as a nice reminder of the algebra of inequalities.

- For some classes, you may prefer the following version of this activity, in which two separate "proofs" are given to the statement 2 > 3:

1. $1/4 > 1/8 \Rightarrow 0.5^2 > 0.5^3 \Rightarrow \log_7 0.5^2 > \log_7 0.5^3 \Rightarrow 2 \log_7 0.5 > 3 \log_7 0.5$
    $\Rightarrow 2 > 3.$

2. $1/4 > 1/8 \Rightarrow 0.5^2 > 0.5^3 \Rightarrow \log_{0.7} 0.5^2 > \log_{0.7} 0.5^3 \Rightarrow 2 \log_{0.7} 0.5 > 3 \log_{0.7} 0.5 \Rightarrow 2 > 3.$

See Also

See also Activity 12.

One Equals Zero and Other Mathematical Surprises ©1998 by Key Curriculum Press

14 A Question of Quadratics

The solution formula for the quadratic equation $ax^2 + bx + c = 0$ is

$$x = \frac{-b \pm \sqrt{b^2 - 4ac}}{2a}.$$

What happens if $a = 0$?

If $a = 0$, the quadratic equation becomes linear, $bx + c = 0$, and its solution is

$$x = \frac{-c}{b}.$$

But when you substitute $a = 0$ into the solution formula, you get

$$x = \frac{-b \pm \sqrt{b^2}}{0} = \frac{-2b}{0} \text{ or } \frac{0}{0},$$

neither of which is meaningful, let alone correct.

What is wrong here?

14

A Question of Quadratics

Explanation

The explanation lies in the derivation of the solution formula:

$$ax^2 + bx + c = 0$$

$$a\left(x^2 + \frac{b}{a}x\right) = -c$$

$$a\left[x^2 + \frac{b}{a}x + \left(\frac{b}{2a}\right)^2\right] = a\left(\frac{b}{2a}\right)^2 - c$$

$$a\left(x + \frac{b}{2a}\right)^2 = \frac{b^2 - 4ac}{4a}$$

$$\left(x + \frac{b}{2a}\right)^2 = \frac{b^2 - 4ac}{4a^2}$$

$$x + \frac{b}{2a} = \pm\sqrt{\frac{b^2 - 4ac}{4a^2}} = \frac{\pm\sqrt{b^2 - 4ac}}{2a}$$

$$x = \frac{-b \pm \sqrt{b^2 - 4ac}}{2a}$$

The crucial point is that in the second and fifth lines we need to assume that $a \neq 0$ because we divide by a. So we obtain the formula under the assumption that $a \neq 0$. Thus, it is not surprising that we fail to find a meaningful solution when we substitute $a = 0$ into the formula.

Comments

- In an alternative form of the formula, we do not need to assume that $a \neq 0$. However, we need to assume that $c \neq 0$. If $c \neq 0$, it is clear that $x \neq 0$, so we can divide throughout by x^2 to get

$$c\left(\frac{1}{x}\right)^2 + b\left(\frac{1}{x}\right) + a = 0 \Leftrightarrow \frac{1}{x} = \frac{-b \pm \sqrt{b^2 - 4ac}}{2c}.$$

We now substitute $a = 0$ into the formula to get $\frac{1}{x} = \frac{-b \pm \sqrt{b^2}}{2c} = 0$, or $\frac{-b}{c}$.

Only one of these two solutions is valid because we have a linear equation if $a = 0$. We may reject the "solution" $\frac{1}{x} = 0$, introduced when we divided by x^2. So, because $\frac{1}{x} \neq 0$, we are left with $\frac{1}{x} = \frac{-b}{c}$ or $x = \frac{-c}{b}$.

- Note that if $c = 0$, the quadratic equation becomes $ax^2 + bx = 0$ and its solution is $x = 0$, or $x = \frac{-b}{a}$.

15 A Fault in the Fractions

Kwan's teacher asked him to find the two solutions of the equation

$$\frac{x^2 - 2x - 3}{x^2 + x + 1} = \frac{x^2 - 2x - 3}{2x^2 + x + 2}.$$

Kwan remembered learning that

> If two fractions are equal and
> their numerators are equal,
> then their denominators are equal.

Because the numerators of the fractions are the same, he equated the denominators:

$$x^2 + x + 1 = 2x^2 + x + 2$$
$$\Leftrightarrow \qquad x^2 + 1 = 0,$$

which has no real solutions.

However, Kwan's teacher said that the equation had two solutions. Where is the flaw in Kwan's argument?

15

A Fault in the Fractions

Explanation

The statement Kwan remembered about two equal fractions was not quite correct. Let's check the details:

If $\quad \dfrac{a}{b} = \dfrac{a}{c}$,

then $\quad ac = ab$

or $\quad a(b - c) = 0.$

So $\quad b = c$, or $a = 0.$

Kwan's memory would have served him better if he had remembered the rule this way:

> If two fractions are equal and
> their numerators are equal *and not zero,*
> then their denominators are equal.

So when he solved the equation $\dfrac{x^2 - 2x - 3}{x^2 + x + 1} = \dfrac{x^2 - 2x - 3}{2x^2 + x + 2}$,

he should not only have looked for solutions by equating the denominators, but should also have considered the possibility that the numerator was zero:

$$x^2 - 2x - 3 = 0$$

$$\Leftrightarrow \quad (x - 3)(x + 1) = 0$$

$$\Leftrightarrow \quad x = 3, \text{ or } x = -1.$$

Comments

- It is correct to say that if two fractions are equal and their denominators are equal, then their numerators are equal—it is not necessary to specify that the denominators are not zero because no fraction can have a zero denominator.

- If we solve the equation $\dfrac{x^2 + 3x - 4}{x^2 - 3x - 2} = \dfrac{x^2 + 3x - 4}{x^2 - 2x - 6}$

by merely equating the denominators, only one solution is found:

$$x^2 - 3x - 2 = x^2 - 2x - 6$$

$$\Leftrightarrow \quad x = 4.$$

However, if we account for the possibility that the numerators are zero, we find two more solutions:

$$x^2 + 3x - 4 = 0$$

$$\Leftrightarrow \quad (x + 4)(x - 1) = 0$$

$$\Leftrightarrow \quad x = -4, \text{ or } x = 1.$$

- The flaw in Kwan's argument boiled down once again to canceling a zero. (See also Activities 1, 7, and 15.) This flaw can be explained as an overgeneralization of such simple cases as $\frac{3}{x} = \frac{3}{2} \Rightarrow x = 2$.

Some students tend to similarly treat the somewhat similar, but different, equation $\frac{x-3}{x-1} = \frac{x-3}{x-2}$. In this case it is not valid to state the following: " $\frac{x-3}{x-1} = \frac{x-3}{x-2} \Leftrightarrow x - 1 = x - 2 \Rightarrow -1 = -2$, which is a contradiction. Hence, there is no solution." Indeed, the contradiction implies that if $x \neq 3$, then there is no other solution. In other words, the only candidate for a solution is $x = 3$. If $x = 3$, then both sides of the equation equal zero. Hence, $x = 3$ is a solution. When we substitute 3 for x in the equation, we do *not* get the contradiction $-1 = -2$. We get $\frac{0}{2} = \frac{0}{1}$.

16 The Largest Prime

As positive integers get larger, the number of candidates for dividing an integer gets larger and the likelihood that at least one of those candidates is indeed a divisor seems to get larger. In other words, as numbers get larger, we would expect an increase in the probability that a particular number is composite. Therefore, it would not be unreasonable to suppose that we could reach some limit beyond which a natural number cannot be a prime. Let's show that 9973 is indeed the largest prime!

Assertion:

The prime number 9973 is the largest prime. In other words, all integers greater than 9973 are composite.

Proof:

It is quite easy to check that 9973 is indeed a prime:

Assume $n > 9973$. Of course, no even values of n are prime. Therefore, it suffices to show that if n is an odd number greater than 9973, it is not prime. Because n is odd, then $\frac{n+1}{2}$ and $\frac{n-1}{2}$ are both integers. Observe that

$$n = \left(\frac{n+1}{2}\right)^2 - \left(\frac{n-1}{2}\right)^2.$$

Therefore, $n = k^2 - m^2$ if k and m are the integers $\frac{n+1}{2}$ and $\frac{n-1}{2}$, respectively. As we know, $n = k^2 - m^2 = (k - m)(k + m)$, which implies that n is a composite number. Q.E.D.[1]

On the other hand, Euclid proved a long time ago that among the positive integers there are infinitely many primes. That is, no matter how far we go along the number line, there must be a prime number beyond the point we have reached. If you find this difficult to believe, read over the following proof and see if you can find a flaw in it. In fact, compare both proofs and see if you can figure out which is false. Of course, both might be false, but it is impossible that neither is false because they support contradicting statements.

Assertion:

There is no largest prime.

---

[1] The basic idea of this proof is adapted from W. M. Patterson III, Reader Reflections, *Mathematics Teacher* (November 1989): 587.

Proof:

The proof is by *reductio ad absurdum,* which in Latin means "proof by contradiction" (you may be more familiar with the term *indirect proof*).

Suppose there *is* a largest prime, beyond which all the natural numbers are composite. Denote it by *P.*

Let $1 < p_1 < p_2 < p_3, \ldots, p_n = P$ be *all* the prime numbers up to *P.* Consider the product *Q* of all these primes.

Now, let us consider $Q + 1$. Can it be a prime? No, because it is larger than *P* and we assumed that *P* is the largest prime. So $Q + 1$ is not a prime. It must, then, have at least one prime factor. However, none of the primes making up *Q* divides $Q + 1$. (Why?) Thus, the composite number $Q + 1$ has a prime factor greater than *P.* But that contradicts the assumption that *P* is the largest prime.

The contradiction is a consequence of the initial assumption that there *is* a largest prime. Therefore, that assumption must be false, hence, there is *no* largest prime. Q.E.D.

16

The Largest Prime

KEY CONCEPTS
- Composite numbers
- Computers in mathematics
- Infinite sets
- Prime numbers
- Proofs, existence

Explanation

The flaw in the proof that 9973 is the largest prime is in the derivation that n is a composite number from the correct decomposition: $n = (k - m)(k + m)$.

This decomposition does *not* imply that n is composite, because $(k - m) = \frac{n+1}{2} - \frac{n-1}{2} = 1$ and $(k + m) = \frac{n+1}{2} + \frac{n-1}{2} = n$.

Hence the decomposition we obtained is the trivial decomposition of *any* integer n, namely $n = n \cdot 1$, which gives no information about whether n is prime or composite.

Comments

- Note that the proof in this activity does not relate to the number 9973 at all and hence may be applied to any prime number, even to a very small one. This fact strongly suggests that there is something wrong in the proof, but it is still important to find out exactly where the proof goes wrong.

- The proof that there are infinitely many primes is based on the construction of the expression $Q + 1$, for which Q is the product of the primes from 2 up to the largest prime, assuming its existence. Under this assumption $Q + 1$ cannot be prime. However, as this assumption is false, an enlightening exercise is to find the first composite number in the sequence of numbers Q_n, formed by adding 1 to the product of the first n consecutive primes:

$$Q_2 = 2 \cdot 3 + 1 = 7$$
$$Q_3 = 2 \cdot 3 \cdot 5 + 1 = 31$$
$$Q_4 = 2 \cdot 3 \cdot 5 \cdot 7 + 1 = 211$$
$$Q_5 = 2 \cdot 3 \cdot 5 \cdot 7 \cdot 11 + 1 = 2311$$
$$Q_6 = 2 \cdot 3 \cdot 5 \cdot 7 \cdot 11 \cdot 13 + 1 = 30{,}031, \text{ and so on.}$$

Each of these numbers leaves a remainder of 1 when divided by the primes from which it is constructed. Therefore, each one of these numbers is either a prime itself, greater than any prime forming it, or it is divisible by some larger prime. The latter is true of 30,031, which is equal to $59 \cdot 509$.

- Here is a nice way to accentuate the effect of the surprising fact that there is an infinite number of primes: Before students begin working on this activity, advise them to conduct a study of the number of primes in a predetermined interval size of, say, 10 or 50 or 100, given the list of primes up to 2000 or so.[2] Challenge students to find large intervals in which no primes occur. Such a study may follow a guess as to the probability of finding a prime number as numbers get larger.

  Students will realize that, in fact, the occurrence of primes decreases. Some students may suggest drawing a sketch of the graph of the cumulative number of primes up to the number n, as a function of n. This graph is an increasing one, but its rate of increase noticeably slows down. (See the following historical background.)

- If we go far enough along the sequence of primes, we can find intervals having no primes as large as we like. Suppose we want to construct an interval of 1000 consecutive composite numbers. One way to do so is to construct the product of the first 1001 integers (namely 1001!) and add to it 2, 3, 4, . . . , 1001 to get 1000 consecutive composite numbers.

Historical Background

In his *Elements* (Book IX, proposition 20) Euclid did not attempt to prove that there are infinitely many primes—in his day mathematicians were cautious about infinity. What Euclid proved is that for any n, there are at least n different prime numbers. His proof is in fact inductive and direct, not by contradiction (indirect). The proof shows that given any finite number of primes, there is always another prime.

Russian mathematician Pafnuti Lvovich Chebyshev (1821–1894) proved that an interval with no primes cannot be too large because between n and $2n$ there must be at least one prime if $n \geq 3$. (For more about Chebyshev, see the historical background in Activity 40.)

The largest prime known as of October 1998 is the Mersenne prime $2^{3021337} - 1$, discovered by Ronald Clarkson in January 1998. This number comprises 2,094,232 digits. Clarkson discovered this new prime by working with hundreds of other people in the Great Internet Mersenne Prime Search project. Mersenne primes are primes of the form $2^n - 1$ and were first investigated by French monk Marin Mersenne (1588–1648). Although many large primes other than Mersenne primes exist, supercomputer companies are interested in Mersenne primes because these companies use the Lucas-Lehmer test, an efficient method for identifying Mersenne primes, to test the efficiency of their hardware and software.

---

[2] For a list of primes, see Albert H. Beiler, *Recreations in the Theory of Numbers,* "The Queen of Mathematics Entertains," Table 84 (Mineola, NY: Dover, 1964): 214–217. For interesting ideas, see John H. Conway and Richard K. Guy, *A Book of Numbers* (New York: Springer/Copernicus, 1996) and David Wells, *The Penguin Book of Curious and Interesting Numbers* (New York: Penguin Books, 1986).

17   The Bedouin Will

An old Bedouin died and left 17 camels to his three sons. His will specified that $\frac{1}{2}$ the camels should go to his eldest son, $\frac{1}{3}$ to his second son, and $\frac{1}{9}$ to his youngest son. His sons could not see how to distribute the camels without cutting some of them up, or selling them and dividing the money, which they did not want to do. So they went to a tribal elder for advice.

The old man thought for a while and then said, "I have 1 camel. I will add it to your 17 to make 18 camels. Now we shall divide them. The eldest son takes $\frac{1}{2}$ the camels, or 9. The second son takes $\frac{1}{3}$, or 6. The youngest son's share is $\frac{1}{9}$, or 2. Because $9 + 6 + 2 = 17$, there is 1 camel left over, so I get my camel back.

How could it be that the tribal elder succeeded in solving a problem the sons (and probably you, too) thought was impossible?

    One Equals Zero and Other Mathematical Surprises ©1998 by Key Curriculum Press

17

The Bedouin Will

Explanation

The tribal elder did not actually execute the will as specified. By getting 9 camels, the eldest son did *not* get $\frac{1}{2}$ of the 17 camels $\left(\frac{9}{17} \neq \frac{1}{2}\right)$, the middle son did not get $\frac{1}{3}$ of the camels $\left(\frac{6}{17} \neq \frac{1}{3}\right)$, and the youngest did not get $\frac{1}{9}$ of the camels $\left(\frac{2}{17} \neq \frac{1}{9}\right)$. Each, in fact, got more than their father specified.

There are two problems with the terms of the will. One problem is that it is not possible to distribute fractions of camels and leave the camels alive. The other is that the fractions specified in the will do not add up to 1 because $\frac{1}{2} + \frac{1}{3} + \frac{1}{9} = \frac{17}{18}$.

The will only talks about $\frac{17}{18}$ of the 17 camels, so $\frac{1}{18}$ of the total 17 camels is not assigned to any of the sons. The solution the tribal elder found makes use of that $\frac{1}{18}$.

Comments

- The solution the tribal elder suggested distributed the camels in the correct ratio because $9:6:2 = \frac{1}{2}:\frac{1}{3}:\frac{1}{9}$, and therefore it could be argued that this was the solution the old Bedouin intended.

- Replacing the discrete inheritance of 17 camels with a continuous one such as 17 kilograms of camel wool eliminates the problem of having to deal with integers only. Dealing with this problem, students may realize that the will granted only $\frac{17}{18}$ of the father's wealth to the sons.

- A simpler version of the same puzzle can be posed with 5 camels, two sons, and a will specifying that one son should receive $\frac{1}{2}$ the camels and the other son $\frac{1}{3}$. Here the inconsistency in the will is obvious—clearly $\frac{1}{2} + \frac{1}{3}$ does not make a whole $\left(\frac{1}{2} + \frac{1}{3} = \frac{5}{6} < 1\right)$. As in this activity, the problem can be solved by adding a camel to make 6. One son receives 3 camels, the other 2, and the remaining camel is returned to its original owner.

- Here is another variation. This time there are 13 camels and a will specifying that $\frac{1}{2}$ should go to the eldest son, $\frac{1}{3}$ to the second son, and $\frac{1}{4}$ to the youngest. If your students worked on the other problems in this activity, they are probably now alert enough to notice that $\frac{1}{2} + \frac{1}{3} + \frac{1}{4} = \frac{13}{12} > 1$.

  The will can be executed by removing 1 camel to leave 12. The oldest son gets 6 camels, and the second son gets 4. The youngest should inherit 3, but there are only 2 left. At this point, the set-aside camel is returned and given to the youngest son. Although each son got a smaller fraction of the total than specified, the sons' inheritances are in the correct ratio because $6:4:3 = \frac{1}{2}:\frac{1}{3}:\frac{1}{4}$.

- Because $\frac{1}{2} + \frac{1}{4} + \frac{1}{6} = \frac{11}{12}$, another version of this activity involves 11 camels to be divided into the fractions $\frac{1}{2}$, $\frac{1}{4}$, and $\frac{1}{6}$.

Challenge your students to find other combinations of three fractions whose numerators are 1 that will give different versions of the problem presented in this activity. In algebraic terms, we are looking for four positive integers a, b, c, d such that $\frac{1}{a} + \frac{1}{b} + \frac{1}{c} = \frac{d-1}{d} = 1 - \frac{1}{d}$, or $\frac{1}{a} + \frac{1}{b} + \frac{1}{c} + \frac{1}{d} = 1$. The number of camels is $d - 1$.

The simplest solution of this equation is $a = b = c = d = 4$. To find all the solutions systematically, observe that each of the four numbers must be greater than 1 so that each reciprocal is less than 1. Now, assume that $1 < a \le b \le c \le d$. Because $\frac{1}{a}$ is the largest reciprocal, $\frac{1}{a} \ge \frac{1}{4}$ or else the sum will be ≤ 1. So $1 < a \le 4$. Let's examine the options for $a = 4$, $a = 3$, or $a = 2$.

$$a = 4 \Rightarrow \frac{1}{b} + \frac{1}{c} + \frac{1}{d} = \frac{3}{4} \Rightarrow b = 4, c = 4, d = 4.$$

$$a = 3 \Rightarrow \frac{1}{b} + \frac{1}{c} + \frac{1}{d} = \frac{2}{3} \Rightarrow b = 3 \text{ or } b = 4.$$

By similar reasoning, $b = 3 \Rightarrow 4 \le c \le 6$, which yields the solutions

$\frac{1}{3} + \frac{1}{3} + \frac{1}{4} = 1 - \frac{1}{12}$ and $\frac{1}{3} + \frac{1}{3} + \frac{1}{6} = 1 - \frac{1}{6}$, and $b = 4 \Rightarrow c = 4$,

which yields the solution $\frac{1}{3} + \frac{1}{4} + \frac{1}{4} = 1 - \frac{1}{6}$.

$$a = 2 \Rightarrow \frac{1}{b} + \frac{1}{c} + \frac{1}{d} = \frac{1}{2} \Rightarrow 2 \le b \le 6.$$

For $b = 2$ there is no solution because the sum of $\frac{1}{a}$ and $\frac{1}{b}$ is 1.

By similar reasoning, we get the following solutions for $b = 3$, $b = 4$, $b = 5$, and $b = 6$:

$b = 3$: $\quad \frac{1}{2} + \frac{1}{3} + \frac{1}{7} = 1 - \frac{1}{42}$, $\frac{1}{2} + \frac{1}{3} + \frac{1}{8} = 1 - \frac{1}{24}$, $\frac{1}{2} + \frac{1}{3} + \frac{1}{9} = 1 - \frac{1}{18}$,

$\quad\quad\quad \frac{1}{2} + \frac{1}{3} + \frac{1}{10} = 1 - \frac{1}{15}$, and $\frac{1}{2} + \frac{1}{3} + \frac{1}{12} = 1 - \frac{1}{12}$;

$b = 4$: $\quad \frac{1}{2} + \frac{1}{4} + \frac{1}{5} = 1 - \frac{1}{20}$, $\frac{1}{2} + \frac{1}{4} + \frac{1}{6} = 1 - \frac{1}{12}$, and $\frac{1}{2} + \frac{1}{4} + \frac{1}{8} = 1 - \frac{1}{8}$;

$b = 5$: $\quad \frac{1}{2} + \frac{1}{5} + \frac{1}{5} = 1 - \frac{1}{10}$;

$b = 6$: $\quad \frac{1}{2} + \frac{1}{6} + \frac{1}{6} = 1 - \frac{1}{6}$.

So, similar problems involve 3, 5, 6, 7, 9, 11, 14, 17, 19, 23, and 41 camels. For cases of 5 and 11 camels there can be a few variations of the distribution of the camels.[3]

Historical Background

The Bedouin Will problem is very old. Similar problems are found in ancient Persian and Indian mathematical writings.

There is even a problem of this type in the *Rhind Mathematical Papyrus,* with 700 loaves of bread to be divided among four men. In the Rhind problem the fractions given are $\frac{2}{3}, \frac{1}{2}, \frac{1}{3}$, and $\frac{1}{4}$, which clearly add up to more than 1. The solution given divides the loaves in four parts proportional to the four fractions. Mathematicians of ancient Egypt used only unit fractions (fractions with numerator of 1), with the sole exception of $\frac{2}{3}$. They expressed all other fractions as sums of unit fractions. The *Rhind Mathematical Papyrus,* discovered by Egyptologist Henry Rhind in 1858, contains a table that expresses fractions of the form $\frac{2}{n}$ in terms of unit fractions for all odd numbers n from 5 to 101. (For example, $\frac{2}{5} = \frac{1}{3} + \frac{1}{15}$.) (The *Rhind Mathematical Papyrus* is also known as the *Ahmes Papyrus* after the Egyptian scribe Ahmes, who in 1650 B.C. copied it from an even earlier document. The papyrus is currently on display in the British Museum in London.)

Italian mathematician Niccoló Fontana (1499–1577) was the first to suggest the solution of the Bedouin Will problem by introducing the extra camel. Fontana, better known by his nickname Tartaglia ("the Stammerer"), is usually remembered for his solution of the general cubic equation and as the founder of the science of ballistics.

---

[3] In general, any n-term equation of reciprocals adding up to 1 has a finite number of solutions: On the one hand, each of the integers must be greater than or equal to 2 or else the sum will include a term $\frac{1}{1}$, which requires that the rest of the reciprocals equal zero, and that is impossible. On the other hand, the largest reciprocal must be greater than or equal to $\frac{1}{n}$ or else the n fractions will add up to a number less than 1. Hence, the smallest integer cannot exceed n. Therefore, the smallest integer is bounded by 2 and n. Setting the n unknown integers in their natural order and starting the analysis from the integer assumed to be the smallest leads necessarily to a finite number of solutions.

18 Discount and Sales Tax

You find an article on a supermarket shelf advertised at a 20% discount. You take it to the cashier, who subtracts 20% from the price and then adds 13% sales tax. You protest, saying that if the 13% sales tax is added before the 20% discount is subtracted, you get a bigger discount and thus pay a smaller amount.

The store manager is called over and disagrees with you, saying that if you subtract the 20% discount first, you pay the 13% sales tax on a lower amount, which is to your advantage.

Which method of calculating the price is better for the customer: adding the tax and then subtracting the discount, or subtracting the discount before adding the tax?

18

Discount and Sales Tax

Explanation

The two methods lead to the same final price for the customer. Suppose the original price of the item is C. If the 20% discount is subtracted before adding the tax, the price becomes $C \cdot \frac{80}{100}$. When 13% sales tax is added, the price becomes $C \cdot \frac{80}{100} \cdot \frac{113}{100}$. On the other hand, if the sales tax is added to the original price first, the price becomes $C \cdot \frac{113}{100}$. When the 20% discount is now subtracted, the net price to the customer is $C \cdot \frac{113}{100} \cdot \frac{80}{100}$. Thus, both final prices are the same.

Comments

- Although the answer is so obvious, many find it difficult to see at first because the words conceal the issue. The way in which the problem is presented clouds the issue by referring to *subtracting* a discount and *adding* sales tax. The issue is clarified by thinking in terms of *multiplication,* using the mathematical expressions shown in the explanation of this activity.

- The explanation amounts to observing that the two methods are the same because multiplication is commutative.

- Percentages are a particular case of fractions. Percentages are fractions whose denominator is 100. Problems similar to that in this activity can be formed with fractions. For example, in Figure 1, which is bigger: one half of a quarter or one quarter of a half?

Figure 1

One-half of a quarter (of a circle)

One-quarter of a half (of a circle)

19

All Men Are Bald

Here is a proof by mathematical induction that all men are bald. You know this is false, so read the proof carefully to see if you can find its error:

Let's agree at the start that any man with absolutely no hair on his head is bald. Let's also agree that a man with just one hair is also bald. Furthermore, a man with just one more hair than a bald man is also bald because one hair cannot make a difference to our idea of baldness.

In other words, if any man with n hairs on his head is bald, so is any other man with $n + 1$ hairs.

Now the usual argument by mathematical induction proves that all men are bald.

Where is the error in this argument?

19

All Men Are Bald

Explanation

There is nothing wrong with the argument. The problem is that *bald* is not a clearly defined term. Obviously a man with no hair is bald, and a man with 3,000,000 hairs is not. But it is a matter of opinion whether a man with only 500 hairs on his head is bald. Baldness can also depend on where the hairs are growing. *Bald* is an ambiguous term, so it cannot be used in a mathematical argument.

Comments

- Using a similar argument, we can "prove" that all natural numbers are interesting. We agree that 1 is interesting. For example, it is the unique multiplicative identity. Suppose now that all numbers up to m are interesting. Then there are two alternatives for $m + 1$: either it is interesting, or it is the first uninteresting number—which makes it interesting! In either case $m + 1$ is interesting, so by mathematical induction all numbers are interesting.

  Again, there is nothing wrong with this proof. If it sounds fishy, that is because the definition of the term *interesting* is vague. Here is another example: Is the property of being the 1736th natural number a unique property of 1736? If so, then we can easily find a reason for seeing any natural number as an interesting number. But common sense does not allow us to do this, because doing so abolishes the intuitive meaning of the word *interesting* in a mathematical context. After all, if *every* natural number is interesting, then *no* natural number is interesting. Some may say that this argument seems to prove that *interesting* is a very uninteresting idea. (Besides, all mathematicians know that all numbers are interesting. They do not need to prove it!)

- The principle of mathematical induction (PMI) states the following: A subset of N that contains 1 and that contains $n + 1$ whenever it contains n must equal N.

  Note that this principle deals with subsets of the set of natural numbers.

  PMI can be applied to proofs of open sentences in the single variable n, $P(n)$. To establish the truth of $P(n)$ for all $n \in N$ (the symbol $\in$ means "belongs to"), we must consider the subset T of N that contains all the truth values of $P(n)$ and we must verify two properties of T:

  1. $1 \in T$, namely, $P(1)$ is true. (Verification of this property is commonly called the checking step.)

2. For any natural number k, if $k \in T$, then $k + 1 \in T$. Namely, for any particular natural number k, the truth of $P(k)$ implies the truth of $P(k + 1)$. (Verification of this property is commonly called the transition step.)

Having successfully verified each one of these properties, we may deduce from PMI that the truth set of $P(n)$ is N, namely, that for all $n \in N$, $P(n)$ is true. (See the historical background in this activity.)

- Some propositions may appear to be provable by PMI because they have the form of an open statement with the variable n. But if the statement to be proved involves an imprecise concept such as "bald," we cannot use PMI to prove it. This activity illustrates that point.

See Also

See also Activity 20.

Historical Background

Italian mathematician Giuseppe Peano (1858–1932) is usually credited with setting up five axioms for the system of natural numbers N:

1. $1 \in N$.

2. If $n \in N$, then $S(n) \in N$ such that S denotes the successor function $S(x) = x + 1$.

3. For no $n \in N$ is $S(n) = 1$.

4. For $n, m \in N$ $S(n) = S(m)$ implies $n = m$.

5. A subset of N that contains 1 and that contains $S(n)$ whenever it contains n must equal N.

The last axiom is known as the principle of mathematical induction (PMI).

20 The Harder Problem Is Easier to Prove

Here is a straightforward proof by mathematical induction that $(1 + x)^n \geq 1 + nx$ for all positive real numbers x and all natural numbers n.

We first note that if $n = 1$, the inequality is clearly satisfied because $(1 + x)^1 \geq 1 + 1 \cdot x$.

Suppose this result is true for some natural number m. We then want to prove that the result also holds for the next natural number, $m + 1$.

We start with the assumption that $(1 + x)^m \geq 1 + mx$ is true.

Multiply both sides by $1 + x$ (which is positive):

Then

$$(1 + x)(1 + x)^m \geq (1 + x)(1 + mx),$$

or

$$(1 + x)^{(m + 1)} \geq 1 + mx + x + mx^2.$$

Now

$$1 + mx + x + mx^2 = 1 + (m + 1)x + mx^2$$
$$\geq 1 + (m + 1)x.$$

Hence

$$(1 + x)^{(m+1)} \geq 1 + (m + 1)x.$$

The result now follows by mathematical induction.

Now consider another problem:

Prove that $(1 + x)^n > nx$ for all positive real numbers x and all natural numbers n.

1. Do you agree that this inequality follows from the inequality given in the proof above? Does this new problem look easier to prove?

2. Try to prove that $(1 + x)^n > nx$ by mathematical induction, using the method shown above. What goes wrong? Can you explain why?

20

The Harder Problem Is Easier to Prove

Explanation

1. Because $1 + nx > nx$ and we proved in the first part of this activity that $(1 + x)^n \geq 1 + nx$, it immediately follows that $(1 + x)^n > nx$. So it certainly looks like the new problem should be easier to prove.

2. The proof by mathematical induction starts, as in the first part of this activity, by checking that the result holds for $n = 1$: $(1 + x)^1 > 1 \cdot x$ is certainly true.

   Now suppose that $(1 + x)^m > mx$ for some m.

   We want to prove that $(1 + x)^{(m+1)} > (m + 1)x$.

   As we did before, we multiply our inequality by $1 + x$ (which is positive):

   $$(1 + x)(1 + x)^m > (1 + x)mx,$$

   giving

   $$(1 + x)^{(m+1)} > mx + mx^2.$$

   Because we are trying to prove that $(1 + x)^{(m+1)} > (m + 1)x$, all we must do now is show that $mx + mx^2 > (m + 1)x$:

   $$mx + mx^2 > (m + 1)x$$
   $$\Leftrightarrow \quad mx + mx^2 > mx + x$$
   $$\Leftrightarrow \quad mx^2 > x$$
   $$\Leftrightarrow \quad mx > 1 \text{ (because } x > 0).$$

   However, this result may not be true, so our attempt has failed.

   The fact that our proof by mathematical induction failed does not mean that our result is false. Indeed, we already know the result is true. The situation presented in this activity is paradoxical because the stronger inequality, $(1 + x)^n \geq 1 + nx$, is easier to prove than the weaker inequality, $(1 + x)^n > nx$.

Comments

- You can gain some insight into the paradox in this activity by considering the crucial inductive step from m to $m + 1$:

  Let P_m denote the proposition $(1 + x)^m > mx$

  and P'_m the proposition $(1 + x)^m \geq 1 + mx$.

The following implications have been established:

$$P'_m \quad \Rightarrow \quad P'_{(m+1)}$$
$$\Downarrow \qquad\qquad \Downarrow$$
$$P_m \qquad\qquad P_{(m+1)}.$$

However, P_m is too weak an assumption from which to obtain the conclusion $P(m+1)$.

- Here are two more examples of inequalities that cannot be proved by straightforward mathematical induction:

1. $\dfrac{1}{1^2} + \dfrac{1}{2^2} + \ldots + \dfrac{1}{n^2} < 2$

2. $\dfrac{1 \cdot 3 \cdot 5 \cdot \ldots \cdot (2n-1)}{2 \cdot 4 \cdot 6 \cdot \ldots \cdot 2n} \leq \dfrac{1}{\sqrt{2n}}$

However, the following stronger inequalities are readily proved by mathematical induction:

1'. $\dfrac{1}{1^2} + \dfrac{1}{2^2} + \ldots + \dfrac{1}{n^2} < 2 - \dfrac{1}{n}$

2'. $\dfrac{1 \cdot 3 \cdot 5 \cdot \ldots \cdot (2n-1)}{2 \cdot 4 \cdot 6 \cdot \ldots \cdot 2n} \leq \dfrac{1}{\sqrt{2n+1}}$

See Also

For another activity related to mathematical induction, see Activity 19.

Historical Background

See Activity 19.

21 The Rising Moon Paradox

Have you ever noticed that when the full moon rises, it appears to be much larger when it is just above the horizon than when it is directly overhead several hours later?

However, the moon is a little farther from you when it is rising than when it is directly overhead!

1. Do you believe this fact?

2. Can you explain why the moon at the horizon seems so much bigger than the moon at its zenith?

Some time later...

21

The Rising Moon Paradox

Explanation

1. It is indeed true that the rising moon is a little farther away from us than when it is at its zenith. To explain this phenomenon, let the radius of the earth be r and let the distance from the moon to the surface of the earth be R, as shown in Figure 1. Let d be the distance from the observer to the rising moon.

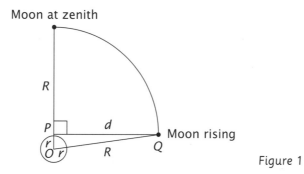

Moon at zenith

Moon rising

Figure 1

Then, because $OP + PQ > OQ$,

$$r + d > r + R,$$

and hence

$$d > R.$$

However, this result cannot account for the noticeable difference in the size of the rising moon at varying points in its path across the sky.

2. An explanation for the seemingly different size of the moon at the horizon and of the moon at its zenith can be given in terms of an optical illusion that psychologists refer to as the Ponzo illusion. In Figure 2, the two circles have the same radius. However, the converging lines make the circle on the right appear larger than the circle on the left.

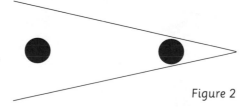

Figure 2

The rising moon paradox can perhaps be explained as a case of the Ponzo illusion rotated 90°, as in Figure 3.

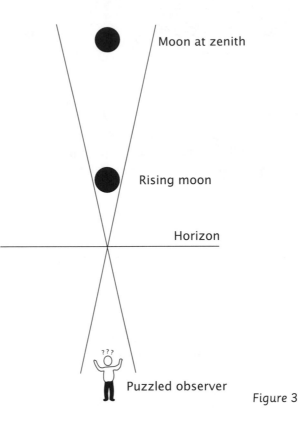

Figure 3

The Ponzo illusion also causes a puzzled observer who is looking down a long tree-lined road to the horizon to think the trees closest to him are much taller than the trees near the horizon.

Comments

- The Ponzo illusion is one of several optical illusions studied by psychologists.[4] In the Müller-Lyon illusion, shown in Figure 4, the horizontal lines are of the same length, but the arrowheads at the ends of the lines lead the eye either inward or outward to create the illusion that one line is longer than the other.

Figure 4

---

[4] A good discussion of optical illusions appears in *Encyclopaedia Britannica,* 15th edition, s.v. "optical illusions."

In the Zöllner illusion, shown in Figure 5, the oblique lines are in fact parallel, but the cross-hatching distorts our perception so that the bottom line appears to tilt toward the top line.

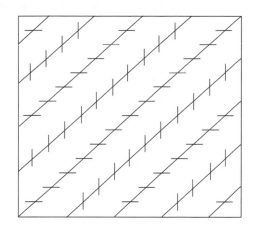

Figure 5

- Optical illusions have psychological, not mathematical, explanations. However, as the illusions shown above illustrate, a number of optical illusions are geometric. This means that students should be careful not to make deductions from geometric figures by relying on the appearances of the figures alone. (For related activities, see Activities 27, 28, 30, 33, 35, and 37.)

22 The Rowboat Paradox

A rowboat is floating in a harbor, and a man is using a long rope to pull the boat toward the harbor wall. When the man has moved 1 meter, how far has the boat moved? Check one of the answers below and provide your reasoning.

____ Exactly 1 meter because:

____ More than 1 meter because:

____ Less than 1 meter because:

One Equals Zero and Other Mathematical Surprises ©1998 by Key Curriculum Press

22

The Rowboat Paradox

Explanation

Most will guess incorrectly that the boat moves less than 1 meter. However, the boat actually moves more than 1 meter. The explanation is a nice little piece of geometry.

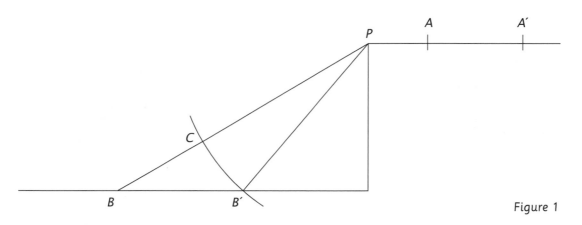

Figure 1

As the man moves from point A to point A', the boat moves from point B to point B', which is the distance in question. In Figure 1, the length of the rope is APB, which equals $A'PB'$. Additionally, $PC = PB'$ and $AA' = 1$ meter, so $BC = 1$ meter.

Because

$$BB' + B'P > BP \text{ (triangle inequality)},$$

we have

$$BB' + B'P > BC + CP.$$

Because

$$B'P = CP,$$

we have

$$BB' > BC = 1 \text{ meter}.$$

23 The Angles of a Triangle

It is a well-known theorem of Euclidean geometry that the sum of the angles of a triangle equals 180°. The proof uses the construction shown in Figure 1:

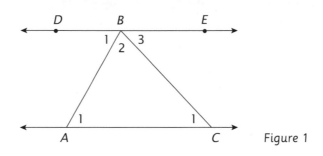

Figure 1

Let ABC be a triangle.

Through point B draw segment DE parallel to segment AC.

Then $\angle A_1 = \angle B_1$ and $\angle C_1 = \angle B_3$ (alternate angles).

Therefore,

$$\angle A_1 + \angle B_2 + \angle C_1 = \angle B_1 + \angle B_2 + \angle B_3 = 180°.$$

Q.E.D.

Now, here is a different proof that does not use a parallel line (see Figure 2):

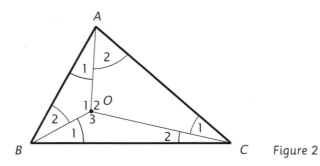

Figure 2

Let ABC be a triangle. Let the sum of the angles be x.

Let's prove that $x = 180°$.

Pick a point O inside the triangle and join the appropriate points to form segments AO, BO, and CO.

$$\angle A_1 + \angle B_2 + \angle O_1 = x \qquad \text{(Sum of the interior angles in } \triangle ABO)$$

$$\angle A_2 + \angle C_1 + \angle O_2 = x \qquad \text{(Sum of the interior angles in } \triangle ACO)$$

$$\angle B_1 + \angle C_2 + \angle O_3 = x \qquad \text{(Sum of the interior angles in } \triangle CBO)$$

Adding gives

$$\angle A_1 + \angle A_2 + \angle B_1 + \angle B_2 + \angle C_1 + \angle C_2 + \angle O_1 + \angle O_2 + \angle O_3 = 3x, \text{ (1)}$$

but

$$\angle O_1 + \angle O_2 + \angle O_3 = 360° \qquad\qquad\qquad\qquad\qquad\qquad (2)$$

and

$$\angle A_1 + \angle A_2 + \angle B_1 + \angle B_2 + \angle C_1 + \angle C_2 = \angle A + \angle B + \angle C = x. \qquad (3)$$

Substituting equations 2 and 3 into equation 1 gives

$$x + 360° = 3x,$$

and it follows that $x = 180°$. Q.E.D.

It is a basic axiom of Euclidean geometry that through a point P not on a line AB there is exactly one line XPY that is parallel to line AB (see Figure 3).

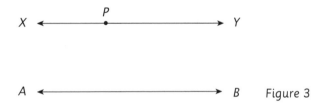

Figure 3

This axiom is often called the parallel postulate and was used in the first proof of this activity.

It is also true that the parallel postulate is logically equivalent to assuming as an axiom that the sum of the angles of a triangle is 180°.

Now, the second proof in this activity does not use the parallel postulate to prove that the sum of the angles of a triangle is 180°. Have we therefore proved the parallel postulate? Or is there an error in the second proof?

KEY CONCEPTS
- *Parallel postulate (Euclid's fifth axiom)*
- *Triangle, sum of the angles of a*

23

The Angles of a Triangle

Explanation

There is nothing wrong with the second proof except that it proves rather less than the theorem states. The proof correctly shows that $x = 180°$, assuming that in any given triangle the angles add up to x such that x is the same for all triangles. What is not proved is that the angle sums of any two triangles are equal. Hence, nothing is wrong with the proof itself, as long as we also prove the constant-sum assertion. To prove this assertion, we need the parallel postulate.

Comment

The important feature of the triangle angle sum theorem is *not* the measure 180°. Rather, it is the fact that this sum is the same for all triangles, no matter how different they are. This fact cannot be established without the parallel postulate.

See Also

See also the second comment in Activity 55. For more on the logical relationships between the parallel postulate and the triangle angle sum theorem, see Activity 24.

Historical Background

From Greek times until the early nineteenth century, the independence of Euclid's fifth axiom within the Euclidean axiom system was long debated. Mathematicians tried to show that the fifth axiom, often called the parallel postulate, was redundant by trying to deduce it as a theorem from Euclid's first four axioms, but such attempts proved either fallacious or circular. On the other hand, no one found a satisfactory way to establish the independence of the axiom. Thus, for centuries it remained questionable whether the parallel postulate was a necessary axiom.

In the Islamic world of the tenth through thirteenth centuries A.D., the concept of parallelism was of great interest to many mathematicians. Numerous attempts were made to prove Euclid's fifth postulate and reformulate his theory of parallel lines. Islamic mathematician Ibn al-Haytham (A.D. 965–1039) reformulated Euclid's theory of parallels by redefining parallel lines as lines that are everywhere equidistant from each other (Euclid defined parallel lines as two lines that nowhere meet). Later, 'Umar ibn Ibrāhīm al-Khayyāmī (A.D. 1048–1122 or 1123), unhappy with his predecessor's proof, set out to prove the parallel postulate through a series of eight propositions based on a quadrilateral with two perpendiculars of equal length. Al-Khayyāmī's approach was more thorough than ibn al-Haytham's because he did not simply hide Euclid's postulate in a new definition but formulated a new postulate. (Al-Khayyāmī is also remembered as poet Omar Khayyam, author of the *Rubaiyat,* a collection of poems immortalized in English translation by nineteenth-century English poet Edward FitzGerald.) About one hundred years after al-Khayyāmī's work, Nasīr al-Dīn al-Tūsī (1201–1274) attempted his own proof of the parallel postulate. His ideas, eventually translated into English and published by English mathematician John Wallis (1616–1703), were studied by many European scholars. In particular, Nasīr al-Dīn's work became the starting point for the developments of Italian mathematician Girolamo Saccheri (1667–1733) and ultimately led to the discovery of alternatives to Euclidean geometry.

In the nineteenth century several mathematicians took courageous steps to resolve the parallel postulate debate by constructing alternatives to Euclidean geometry. These new geometries were based on the first four Euclidean axioms and a fifth axiom that assumes, contrary to Euclid's parallel postulate, that through a point outside a given line there is *no* parallel to the line or there are at least two. Surprisingly, such geometries were found to have a realizable Euclidean model—the former on a sphere, the latter on a hyperboloid—and thus the independence of Euclid's fifth axiom was established. The new geometries came to be called *non-Euclidean geometries,* a term usually credited to German mathematician Carl Friedrich Gauss (1777–1855). Indeed, Gauss was probably the first to anticipate their existence.

A former student of Gauss', German mathematician Georg Friedrich Bernhard Riemann (1826–1866), replaced Euclid's parallel postulate with the assumption that through a given point outside a line, *no* parallel to the line exists. In other words, any two lines in the plane intersect each other. Riemann established the consistency of his assumption with the first four Euclidean axioms, relative to the consistency of Euclid's axiom system, by interpreting them in a model that embodied his new set of five axioms as true Euclidean properties of that model. In Riemann's geometry the model for a plane is the surface of a sphere. A "(straight) line" in Riemannian geometry is then an arc of a great circle, that is, a circle centered at the center of the sphere. Thus through a point outside a line, *no* line exists that does not cross the line. (Note the difference between a circle centered within the sphere and other circles on the surface of the sphere.) Today, Riemann's geometry is known as spherical geometry or elliptic geometry, and is most applicable to astronomy, navigation, geodesy, geography, and other earth sciences.[5]

Two other pioneers in the field of non-Euclidean geometry were Russian mathematician Nikolai Ivanovich Lobachevsky (1792–1856) and Hungarian mathematician

---

[5] For more about spherical geometry, see István Lénárt, *Non-Euclidean Adventures on the Lénárt Sphere*™ (Berkeley, CA: Key Curriculum Press, 1996).

Janós Bolyai (1802–1860). Independently, both developed a geometry assuming, in addition to Euclid's first four axioms, that through a point outside a line, there are at least two lines parallel to the line. Today, the geometry they developed is known as hyperbolic geometry and, like spherical geometry, has numerous practical applications.[6]

---

[6] For an explanation of the term *hyperbolic geometry,* see Richard Courant and Herbert Robbins, *What Is Mathematics?* (New York: Oxford University Press, 1948): 226. For information about Henri Poincaré (1854–1912), his non-Euclidean model, and its application to visual space, see Howard Eves, *Great Moments in Mathematics After 1650* (Washington, DC: Mathematical Association of America, 1982): 82.

24 Walking Around a Triangle

Here is a practical way of convincing yourself that the angles of a triangle add up to 180°.

Imagine yourself standing at vertex *A* of triangle *ABC*, which is labeled clockwise. You are facing along side *AB* toward point *B*. Set out walking toward point *B*. When you get to point *B*, turn counterclockwise through ∠*B*. You now have your back toward point *C*. Walk backwards to point *C*. At point *C*, turn counterclockwise through ∠*C* so that you are now facing toward point *A*. Walk to point *A*, and at point *A* turn counter-clockwise through ∠*A*. You are now standing with your back toward point *B*.

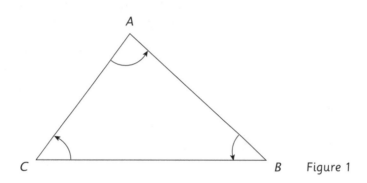

Figure 1

You started off facing toward point *B*. During your journey you passed successively through ∠*B*, ∠*C*, and ∠*A*, each time turning counterclockwise, and you ended up facing the opposite direction. Therefore, you conclude that the total number of degrees you turned must be 180.

Not so fast. How can you be sure that your total rotation does not equal 540°, or 900°, or some other odd multiple of 180°? Rotating these numbers of degrees would also have left you facing opposite point *B*. However, because only once on your journey around the triangle did you actually look into the triangle (during your turn at point *C*), you can indeed conclude that your total rotation equaled no more than 180°.

You can carry out this activity physically, but it is what the Greeks of antiquity would have described as a "thought experiment"—you do not have to do it to be convinced of its validity. Indeed, the argument regarding your amount of rotation is very convincing. The interesting feature of the argument is that it seems to avoid using the parallel postulate, which would make the triangle angle sum theorem logically independent of the parallel postulate. However, the theorem that the sum of the angles of a triangle is 180° is known to be logically equivalent to the parallel postulate. Have you therefore proved the parallel postulate? Is there a paradox in the argument? If so, where is it?

KEY CONCEPTS
- Geometry, spherical
- Parallel postulate (Euclid's fifth axiom)
- Triangle, sum of the angles of a

24

Walking Around a Triangle

Explanation

Unfortunately, or perhaps fortunately, the answer is no, we have not proved the parallel postulate. The hidden assumption in our "walking proof" is that no change in direction took place while we were walking along the sides of the triangle. If in fact our walk took place on the surface of a sphere, where the sides of the triangle are great circles, we would have constantly changed direction during each of the three trips along the sides. The three rotations at the vertices of the spherical triangle would have taken place in different planes, so we could not simply add them together at the end to give our total rotation.

In the plane the assumption that the total rotation is the simple sum of the rotations at the three vertices amounts to assuming that the three angles can be translated to one point and added together. This is precisely the idea behind the proof that involves drawing a line parallel to line BC through point A.

Using the fact that segment BC and line PAQ are parallel, it follows that $\angle A + \angle B + \angle C = \angle CAB + \angle BAQ + \angle PAC = 180°$. To add the angles together and show that they make a straight angle, we need to move them to the point at which they share the same vertex and join their rays without any extra rotation, as shown in Figure 2. To do so, we need the parallel postulate.

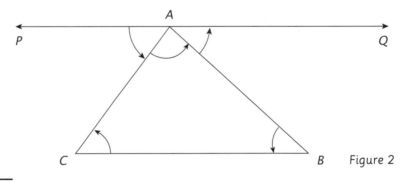

Figure 2

Comment

Invite students to act out this activity so they can see how this process of turning works.

See Also

For more on the logical relationships between the parallel postulate and the triangle angle sum theorem, see Activity 23.

Historical Background

See Activity 23.

25 Congruency Paradox

Do you agree with the following statement? If two triangles have five congruent parts—three sides and two angles, or two sides and three angles—then they are congruent.

It is certainly true that two triangles with three pairs of sides with equal measure are congruent. This is known as SSS congruency. It seems reasonable that three angles and two sides will also generate congruency. Does it?

Consider the example shown in Figure 1:

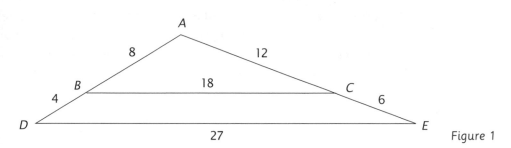

Figure 1

Because $\frac{AB}{BD} = \frac{AC}{CE} = 2$, segments BC and DE are parallel by the proportional intercept theorem. Therefore, triangles ABC and ADE are equiangular. Furthermore, $AC = AD$ and $BC = AE$. Thus, the triangles have five equal parts of equal measure, but they are not congruent!

Can you explain why?

25

Congruency Paradox

KEY CONCEPTS
- Distorting theorems
- Golden ratio
- Triangle congruency
- Triangle inequality
- Triangle similarity

Explanation

The statement "If two triangles have five congruent parts—three sides and two angles, or two sides and three angles—then they are congruent" is false, as the example proves. A minor, yet significant, change turns it into a true statement: "If two triangles have five *corresponding* congruent parts—three sides and two angles, or two sides and three angles—then they are congruent." In the example, the equal parts do not correspond, and as the example proves, congruency does not necessarily follow under such conditions.

Indeed, the statement is true even if "five" is replaced with "four." However, "four" cannot be replaced with "three" because three angles are not sufficient to determine congruency; neither are two sides and an angle. Only particular sets of three *corresponding* congruent parts suffice to determine congruency, for example, three sides (usually abbreviated SSS), two sides and the included angle (usually abbreviated SAS), and two angles and the side opposite the larger angle (usually abbreviated AAS).

Comments

- Congruency rules are generally abbreviated so that they refer only to three sides (SSS), two angles and a side (AAS), and so on. This convention omits a crucial feature of congruency rules: congruent parts must *correspond*. This omission may explain why many students find the type of problem in this activity perplexing. (For another activity based on similar distortions of theorems, see Activity 36.)[7]

- You may find the following example useful for illustrating that equal parts are not necessarily corresponding parts:

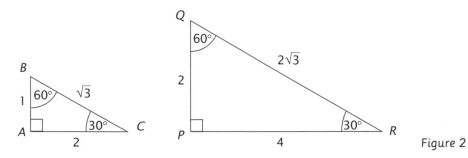

Figure 2

---

[7] For more examples of this type of problem, see N. Movshovitz-Hadar, S. Inbar, and O. Zaslavsky, "Students' Distortions of Theorems," *FOCUS on Learning Problems in Mathematics* 8, no. 1 (1986): 49–57.

In the triangles shown in Figure 2, $\angle B = \angle Q$, $\angle C = \angle R$, and $AC = PQ$, but the parts of the triangles do not correspond.

- This activity focuses attention on the important role the correspondence condition plays in triangle congruency (and similarity). If you implement the following suggested activities, this activity can also serve as a nice reminder of the triangle inequality property.

- You can present the paradox in this activity more openly by posing the question, "Are there any two noncongruent triangles that have five congruent parts?" (Try not to give away any information with nonverbal gestures or your tone of speech.)

It is very likely that the majority of the class will say no. Support this incorrect answer with the following argument: Three parts suffice to establish congruency. Five is greater than three, so among the five parts there must be three that satisfy one of the congruency conditions.

Then, to challenge students to back up their answer with an indirect proof, say, "Suppose for the sake of argument that there *are* two such triangles. Then this presumably false assumption must yield some absurdity." The discourse could take the following path:

The five congruent parts cannot consist of three sides (and two angles) because this contradicts the SSS congruency theorem. Therefore, the triangles must have three congruent angles (and two sides), which means that the triangles must be similar. (Note that the congruency of three angles and two sides does *not* imply a conflict with the ASA congruency theorem or the SAS congruency theorem!)

Label the vertices of the two triangles A, B, C, D, E, and F such that $\angle A = \angle D$, $\angle B = \angle E$, $\angle C = \angle F$, and $AB : DE = BC : EF = CA : FD = m : n$, and suppose triangle ABC is the smaller triangle, namely, $m < n$, as shown in Figure 3.

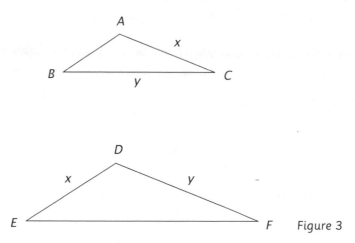

Figure 3

Because only two of the three sides in each triangle have a match in the other one, the smallest side in the smaller triangle and the largest side in the larger triangle cannot have a match. Accordingly, by the similarity of the triangles, we get the following equations:

$$AB : x = x : y = y : EF \Rightarrow AB = x^2 : y, \; EF = y^2 : x.$$

We must add two more restrictions to these two equations: $AB + x > y$, and $x + y > EF$.

Among other measures, $AB = 8$, $x = 12$, $y = 18$, and $EF = 27$ satisfy these conditions. Hence, two triangles that satisfy our initial assumption have sides that measure 8, 12, 18 and 12, 18, 27. There are infinitely many others, of course, and they all agree with our initial assumption.

In searching for a contradiction of our initial assumption, we have arrived at a situation that is consistent with the assumption and shows that all the conditions can in fact be fulfilled.

- A nice follow-up activity is to find more pairs of noncongruent triangles that have five congruent parts (there are infinitely many). A simple way to do so is to multiply the sequence given above (8, 12, 18, 27, . . .) by any whole number greater than 1. For example, the geometric sequence 16, 24, 36, 54, . . . also yields pairs of triangles with five congruent parts.

Another way to find more pairs is to extend the geometric sequence that has the ratio $x : y$ between any two consecutive elements, $\ldots, \frac{y^2}{x}, y, x, \frac{x^2}{y}, \ldots$, to get $\ldots, \frac{y^4}{x^3}, \frac{y^3}{x^2}, \frac{y^2}{x}, y, x, \frac{x^2}{y}, \frac{x^3}{y^2}, \frac{x^4}{y^3}, \ldots$. Any four consecutive elements a, b, c, and d in this sequence can form the sides of the two triangles a, b, c, and b, c, d provided that we choose values for x and y that respect the triangle inequality property. There is a connection here with the golden ratio, as explained in the following comment.

Further restrictions, such as whole numbers for all sides or a unit segment plus another segment given to start with, will make this follow-up activity more challenging.

- Another related problem is to find the relative relations between the size of x and of y. To solve this problem, we observe two facts that stem from the triangle inequality in the smaller triangle:

1. $x + y > \frac{x^2}{y} \Rightarrow y^2 + xy - x^2 > 0.$

   Solving for y gives $y > \frac{-x + \sqrt{x^2 + 4x^2}}{2} \Rightarrow y > x\left(\frac{-1 + \sqrt{5}}{2}\right).$

2. $x + \frac{x^2}{y} > y \Rightarrow y^2 - xy - x^2 < 0.$

   Solving for y gives $y < \frac{x + \sqrt{x^2 + 4x^2}}{2} \Rightarrow y < x\left(\frac{1 + \sqrt{5}}{2}\right).$

   Combining these two results gives $x\left(\frac{-1 + \sqrt{5}}{2}\right) < y < x\left(\frac{1 + \sqrt{5}}{2}\right).$

   Now, $\frac{1 + \sqrt{5}}{2}$ is the golden ratio, denoted by $\varnothing$, and satisfies $\varnothing - 1 = \frac{1}{\varnothing} = \frac{\sqrt{5} - 1}{2}.$

Thus, we have the inequality $\frac{1}{\phi} < \frac{y}{x} < \phi \Rightarrow 0.7 < \frac{y}{x} < 1.6$.

The example in the second comment of this activity uses $\frac{y}{x} = 1.5$.

- Note that there is no case of two noncongruent isosceles triangles having five congruent parts.

- For still another activity related to pairs of triangles whose side measures can be expressed as a, ar, ar^2 and ar, ar^2, ar^3 such that $a > 0$ and $1 < r < \frac{1 + \sqrt{5}}{2}$, see Maurice Burke's *5-Con Triangles*.[8]

---

[8] Maurice Burke, *5-Con Triangles* (National Council of Teachers of Mathematics *Student Math Notes*) (January 1990).

26 Every Trapezoid Is a Parallelogram

A parallelogram is a quadrilateral with both pairs of opposite sides parallel. A trapezoid is a quadrilateral with exactly one pair of parallel sides.

Claim:

All trapezoids are parallelograms.

Proof:

Let *ABCD* be a trapezoid with segment *AD* parallel to segment *BC*, *AD* = *a*, and *BC* = *b*. Extend segment *DA* to point *F* so that *AF* = *b*, and extend segment *BC* to point *E* so that *CE* = *a*. Join segments *FE*, *AC*, and *BD*, as shown in Figure 1.

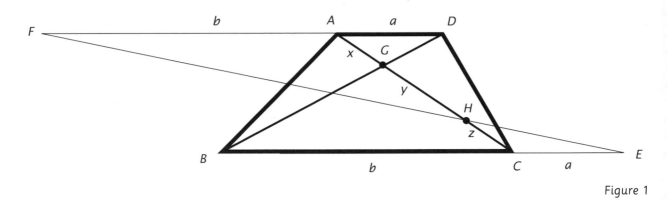

Figure 1

Let the diagonals of the trapezoid, *AC* and *BD*, meet at point *G* and let segments *AC* and *FE* meet at point *H*. Let *AG* = *x*, *GH* = *y*, and *HC* = *z*.

Then, because triangles *AGD* and *CGB* are similar,

$$\frac{a}{b} = \frac{x}{y+z} \Rightarrow x = \frac{a}{b} \cdot (y+z). \qquad (1)$$

Because triangles *AHF* and *CHE* are similar,

$$\frac{a}{b} = \frac{z}{x+y} \Rightarrow z = \frac{a}{b} \cdot (x+y). \qquad (2)$$

Subtracting equation 2 from equation 1 gives

$$x - z = \frac{a}{b}(z - x)$$

$$\frac{a}{b} = -1 \Rightarrow |a| = |b|.$$

Thus, *AD* = *BC* and *ABCD* is a parallelogram. Q.E.D.

Where is the flaw in the proof?

One Equals Zero and Other Mathematical Surprises ©1998 by Key Curriculum Press

26

Every Trapezoid Is a Parallelogram

KEY CONCEPTS
- Dividing by zero
- Parallelograms
- Proportional segments
- Quadrilaterals
- Trapezoids
- Triangle similarity

Explanation

The logical development of the proof is correct up to $\frac{a}{b} = -1$. This step must be wrong, because a and b are lengths and thus possess positive values. The flaw arose at the previous step, when $z - x$ was canceled, because the possibility that $x = z$ was ignored.

Thus the paradox disappears, leaving an exercise on similarity: Prove that in the figure $AG = HC$.

Comments

- We can prove that $z = x$ by applying the proportional segments theorem to triangles *FDB* and *FEB,* relying on the fact that *AFBC* is a parallelogram:

Segment *AC* parallel to segment *FB* implies in triangle *FDB* that

$$\frac{x}{FB} = \frac{a}{a + b}$$

and in triangle *FEB* that

$$\frac{z}{FB} = \frac{a}{a + b}.$$

It follows that

$$x = z.$$

- We usually face the need to avoid dividing by zero in the course of learning how to solve equations. The paradox in this activity provides a geometric and, hence, an unusual angle on this issue. (See also Activities 1, 3, and 14.)

- You can take this opportunity to discuss the definition of a trapezoid. A trapezoid can be defined as a quadrilateral that has *at least* one pair of parallel opposite sides. In this definition parallelograms become particular cases of trapezoids. If we define trapezoids as quadrilaterals that have *just* one pair of parallel sides, then parallelograms do not form a subset of trapezoids. (Note that stating "a quadrilateral that has one pair"—without saying "at least" or "just"—means "at least one pair.") The former definition seems to be more natural because any theorem that applies to trapezoids and that does not require just one pair of parallel sides will also apply to parallelograms.

27 Every Triangle Is Isosceles

The following arguments apparently prove that all triangles are isosceles. Read each argument carefully, filling in the missing details.

Argument 1:

Refer to Figure 1. Let *ABC* be a triangle. Let the bisector of ∠*A* meet the perpendicular bisector of segment *BC* at point *O*. Let points *P*, *Q*, and *R* be the feet of the perpendiculars from point *O* to segments *BC*, *CA*, and *AB* respectively.

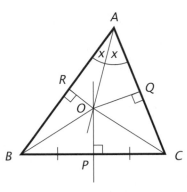

Figure 1

1. Prove that triangles *ARO* and *AQO* are congruent and deduce that
   OR = OQ and *AR = AQ*.

2. Prove that *OB = OC*.

3. Prove that triangles *BOR* and *COQ* are congruent and deduce that
   BR = CQ.

4. Add the equations *AR = AQ* and *BR = CQ* to obtain *AB = AC*.

Argument 2:

Figure 2 shows another interpretation of the figure described in Argument 1.

In this modified figure, segments *AO* and *PO* appear to meet outside triangle *ABC*, and points *R* and *Q* lie on extended segments *AB* and *AC*, respectively. Repeat the steps given in Argument 1, referring this time to Figure 2. Only one small change is needed in step 4 to reach the same conclusion reached in Argument 1: *AB = AC*.

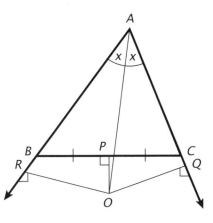

Figure 2

Where is the error in each of these arguments?

 One Equals Zero and Other Mathematical Surprises ©1998 by Key Curriculum Press

KEY CONCEPTS
- Angle bisectors
- Angles, circumferential
- Perpendicular bisectors
- Proofs
- Relying on figures
- Triangles, isosceles

27

Every Triangle Is Isosceles

Explanation

Argument 1:

1. Triangles *ARO* and *AQO* are congruent because ∠*RAO* = ∠*QAO* (segment *AO* bisects ∠*A*), ∠*ARO* = ∠*AQO* = 90° (construction), and segment *AO* is the common side of the triangles. The triangles are congruent (two angles and a side), and hence *OR* = *OQ* and *AR* = *AQ*.

2. Because points on the perpendicular bisector of a line segment are equidistant from the endpoints of the segment, *OB* = *OC*. Alternately, triangles *OPB* and *OPC* can be proved congruent (two sides and an included angle).

3. Triangles *BOR* and *COQ* are congruent because *OB* = *OC* (see step 2), *OR* = *OQ* (see step 1), and ∠*BRO* = ∠*CQO*. The triangles are congruent (hypotenuse and side of a right-angled triangle), and hence *BR* = *CQ*.

4. *AB* = *AR* + *RB* = *AQ* + *QC* = *AC*.

Argument 2:

The only modification needed is in step 4: *AB* = *AR* − *RB* = *AQ* − *QC* = *AC*.

Error:

The fallacy lies in the positions of the feet of the perpendiculars. It is correct that point *O*, the intersection of the bisector of ∠*A* and the perpendicular bisector of segment *BC*, lies outside the triangle, although it is not quite obvious why. The reason is that point *O* will lie on the circumcircle of the triangle, for if the circumcircle is drawn, as in Figure 3, and the perpendicular bisector of *BC* is constructed outward to meet the circumcircle at point *O*, then *OB* = *OC* (as we have observed). Hence, the angles that these equal chords subtend at point *A* will be equal. Therefore, segment *OA* is the bisector of ∠*A*.

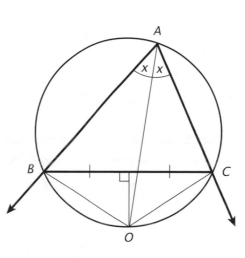

Figure 3

Thus, the figure in Argument 2 is more correct than the figure in Argument 1. The crucial point now is the location of the feet of the perpendiculars dropped from point *O* to *AB* and *AC*. A careful construction suggests that one of the feet lies inside the triangle and the other lies outside.

We now have either Figure 4 or Figure 5:

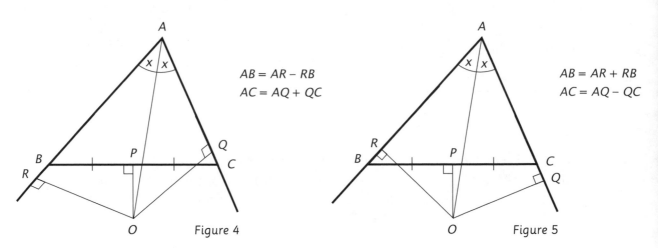

$AB = AR - RB$
$AC = AQ + QC$

Figure 4

$AB = AR + RB$
$AC = AQ - QC$

Figure 5

Although $AR = AQ$ and $RB = QC$ in both figures, it is not possible to add or subtract the equations to obtain the paradoxical $AB = AC$. Note that the figure on the left cannot be correctly drawn; the argument above shows why this is impossible.

Comments

- The use of "accurate constructions" to establish which figure is correct is unsatisfactory. In fact, it is possible to prove that, when perpendiculars are dropped from point O (the point on the circumcircle at which the bisector of $\angle A$ and the perpendicular bisector of segment BC meet), the feet of the three perpendiculars will be collinear. (The line on which the three feet lie is called the Simson line.) The proof is not difficult and uses properties of cyclic quadrilaterals.

In Figure 6, $ABOC$ is cyclic by construction, as are $PBRO$ (opposite angles are supplementary) and $OPQC$ (equal angles subtended by OC).

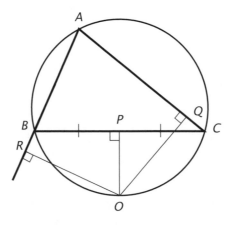

Figure 6

Therefore

$$\angle RPO + \angle OPQ = \angle RBO + \angle OPQ \qquad \text{(Cyclic quad } RBPO\text{)}$$

$$= \angle RBO + (180° - \angle QCO) \qquad \text{(Cyclic quad } PQCO\text{)}$$

$$= \angle ACO + 180° - \angle QCO \qquad \text{(Cyclic quad } ABOC\text{)}$$

$$= 180°.$$

This proves that RPQ is a straight line.

Because in our original argument P was the midpoint of segment BC and RPQ is a straight line, either point R lies between points A and B and point Q lies on AC extended, or point R lies on AB extended and point Q lies between points A and C (see Figure 7).

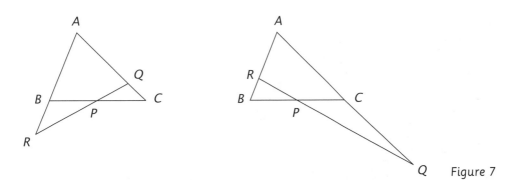

Figure 7

- The fact that a straight line drawn through an interior point of one side of a triangle must cut one side externally and the third internally (or else pass through a vertex) is a necessary axiom of geometry, known as Pasch's axiom. Euclid did not identify the need for such an axiom.

- The role of a figure in a mathematical proof is to help us form a mental image of the various relationships among parts of the data. Sometimes, however, figures can be more misleading than helpful.

See Also

See also Activities 21, 28, 30, 33, 35, and 37.

28 All Obtuse Angles Are Right Angles

Let ∠*ABC* be an obtuse angle, that is, an angle that measures between 90° and 180°.

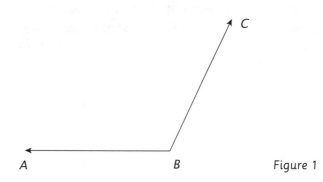

Figure 1

Let's prove that ∠*ABC* = 90°! Watch very carefully:

Assume that *AB* = *BC*.

We construct a square *ABDE* and join points *E* and *C* to form segment *EC*, as shown in Figure 2.

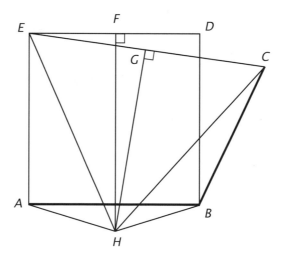

Figure 2

We let the perpendicular bisectors *FH* and *GH* of segments *ED* and *EC*, respectively, meet at point *H*. We then join the appropriate points to form segments *AH, BH, EH,* and *CH*.

In triangles *HAE* and *HBC*

$$AE = BC \qquad\qquad (BD = BC, \text{ and } ABDE \text{ is a square.})$$

$$HA = HB \qquad (HF \text{ is the perpendicular bisector of } AB.)$$

$$EH = CH. \qquad (HG \text{ is the perpendicular bisector of } EC.)$$

Therefore, triangles *HAE* and *HBC* are congruent (three sides),

and hence

$$\angle HAE = \angle HBC.$$

But

$$\angle HAB = \angle HBA. \qquad\qquad (\text{Triangle } HAB \text{ is isosceles.})$$

Subtracting,

$$\angle HAE - \angle HAB = \angle HBC - \angle HBA,$$

so we have

$$90° = \angle ABC.$$

Did you spot the mistake in this argument?

28

All Obtuse Angles Are Right Angles

KEY CONCEPTS
- Angles
- Proofs
- Rectangles
- Relying on figures
- Triangles, congruent

Explanation

The mistake lies in the figure. There are two possible constructions of the figure, only one of which was considered in the activity. The other is shown in Figure 3.

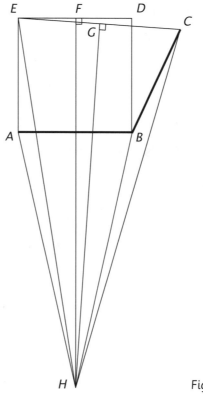

Figure 3

We can use the argument in the activity to show that triangles *HAE* and *HBC* are congruent so that

$$\angle HAE = \angle HBC.$$

Also,

$$\angle HAB = \angle HBA.$$

Subtracting now gives

$$90° = \angle BAE = \angle HBC - \angle HBA,$$

but because ∠*HBA* does not lie inside ∠*HBC,* we cannot deduce that

$$\angle HBC - \angle HBA = \angle ABC.$$

Comments

- Deceptive figures are the basis for several geometric paradoxes. Examples like that given in this activity caution against relying on figures, which may not depict relationships accurately enough. (See also Activities 21, 27, 30, 33, 35, and 37.)

- Even before starting the proof, it is possible to see that Figure 2 in the activity is incorrect. The correct and incorrect figures are shown in Figure 4 for comparison. In both, points *H* and *D* and points *D* and *C* are joined to form segments *HD* and *DC,* respectively.

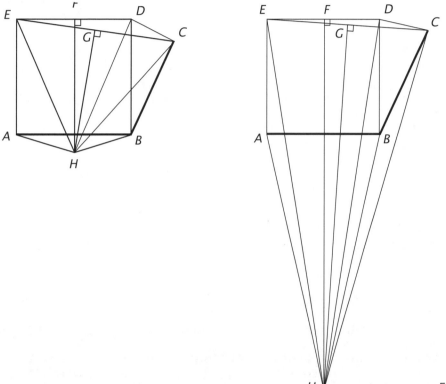

Figure 4

Look at triangles *HDC* and *BDC.* It is an easy exercise to prove that both are isosceles triangles that share the base *DC.* Moreover, *HD > BD,* so clearly point *B* lies inside triangle *HDC.* Therefore, only the second figure can be correct.

29 Two Perpendiculars?

Is it possible to have two perpendiculars from the same point to the same line? Yes it is—if you can believe the following argument:

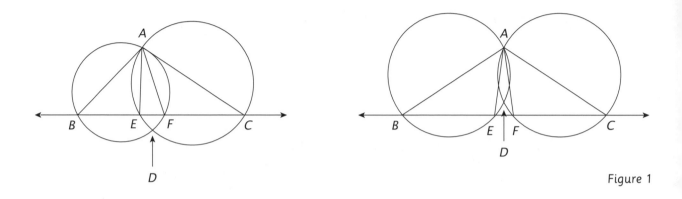

Figure 1

Two circles, with diameters *AB* and *AC,* intersect at points *A* and *D.* Line *BC* cuts the circles at points *E* and *F.* (Figure 1 shows two possibilities.)

Then, in both versions of Figure 1,

$$\angle AEC = 90° \qquad \text{(Angle in semicircle with diameter } AC\text{)}$$

$$\angle AFB = 90°, \qquad \text{(Angle in semicircle with diameter } AB\text{)}$$

giving two perpendiculars (*AE* and *AF*) from point *A* to segment *BC.*

How can this be?

29

Two Perpendiculars?

Explanation

There is nothing wrong with the argument as far as it goes. The problem is that it has not gone far enough. A third possibility is shown in Figure 2, in which points *D*, *E*, and *F* coincide.

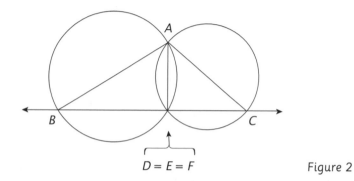

Figure 2

Because the first two cases in this argument led to the erroneous conclusion that it is possible to have two distinct perpendiculars from the same point to the same line, we find that the third case must be the only correct possibility. What we have in fact proved is that if two circles with diameters *AB* and *AC* intersect at points *A* and *D*, then point *D* lies on segment *BC*.

Comment

Here is a similar argument apparently showing that a circle can have two distinct diameters from the same point on its circumference (see Figure 3).

Let *D* be a point inside ∠*ABC*, with perpendiculars *DE* and *DF* dropped to lines *BA* and *BC*, respectively. Then points *D*, *E*, and *F* cannot be collinear.

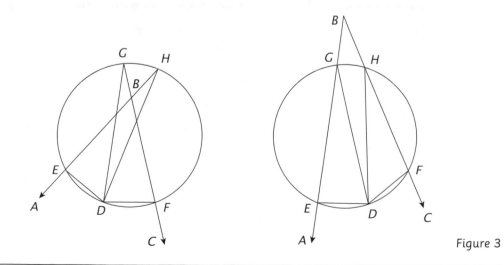

Figure 3

Draw a circle through points *D, E,* and *F,* and let points *G* and *H* be the other intersection points of lines *AB* and *BC* (extended if necessary). Then, in each case

$$DG \text{ is a diameter} \qquad (\text{Because } \angle DFC = 90°)$$

and

$$DH \text{ is a diameter.} \qquad (\text{Because } \angle DEH = 90°)$$

Thus there are two diameters at point *D.* Or are there?

30 The Empty Circle

Let *P* be any point, other than the center, inside a circle with center *O* and radius *r*. Thus, 0 < *OP* < *r*. Let's prove that point *P* lies on the circumference of the circle and hence that, apart from the center, every circle is empty!

Join points *O* and *P* as shown in Figure 1 to create segment *OP*. Then extend *OP* to a point *Q* such that $OP \cdot OQ = r^2$. Let *R* be the midpoint of *PQ*.

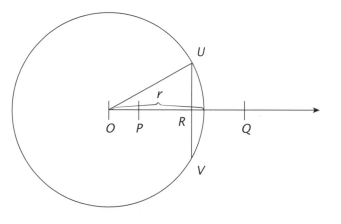

Figure 1

Let *UV* be the chord perpendicular to segment *PQ* at point *R*.

Then

$$OP = OR - RP$$

and

$$OQ = OR + RQ = OR + RP.$$ (Because *RQ* = *RP*)

Therefore,

$$r^2 = OP \cdot OQ$$ (By construction)

$$= (OR - RP)(OR + RP)$$

$$= OR^2 - RP^2$$

$$= (r^2 - RU^2) - (PU^2 - RU^2)$$ (By the Pythagorean theorem)

$$= r^2 - PU^2.$$

Thus, the length of segment *PU* is 0, which means that points *P* and *U* are the same. Thus point *P* lies on the circumference of the circle. Q.E.D.

Is every circle indeed empty?

KEY CONCEPTS
- Arithmetic-mean–
  geometric-mean theorem
- Circles
- Exterior points
- Interior points
- Pythagorean theorem
- Relying on figures

30

The Empty Circle

Explanation

Figure 1 was drawn with the midpoint R of segment PQ inside the circle. If point R is outside the circle, line URV cannot be drawn and the "proof" falls apart.

We could have foreseen the fact that point R must lie outside the circle:

$$OR = \frac{OP + OQ}{2} > \sqrt{OP \cdot OQ}. \quad \text{(Arithmetic-mean–geometric-mean inequality)}$$

But

$$OP \cdot OQ = r^2. \quad \text{(By construction)}$$

Thus

$$OR > r,$$

that is, point R lies outside the circle.

Comments

- The arithmetic-mean–geometric-mean (AM-GM) inequality states that if a_1, a_2, ..., a_n are nonnegative real numbers, then

$$\frac{a_1 + a_2 + \ldots + a_n}{n} \geq \sqrt[n]{a_1 a_2 \cdot \ldots \cdot a_n}$$

and equality holds if and only if $a_1 = a_2 = \ldots = a_n$.

As applied in the activity, $a_1 = OP$, $a_2 = OQ$, and $OP \neq OQ$.

- The proof of the AM-GM inequality for $n = 2$ is quite simple:

$$\frac{a_1 + a_2}{2} - \sqrt{a_1 \cdot a_2} = \frac{1}{2}\left(a_1 - 2\sqrt{a_1 \cdot a_2} + a_2\right)$$

$$= \frac{1}{2}\left(\sqrt{a_1} - \sqrt{a_2}\right)^2$$

$$\geq 0,$$

and equality is true if and only if $a_1 = a_2$.

There are several different proofs for $n > 2$, but none are as easy as this.

- Two points, *P* and *Q,* lying on the same ray from the center of a circle of radius *r* such that $OP \cdot OQ = r^2$ are said to be *inverse* to each other with respect to the circle (see Figure 2). This relationship is the starting point of inversive geometry.[9]

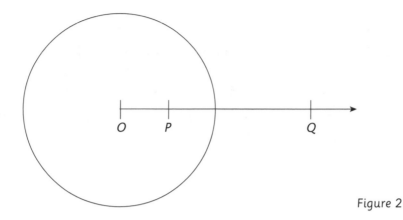

Figure 2

- Several geometric paradoxes depend on deceptive figures. To examine the reliability of a figure, it is sometimes helpful to look at a particular case. Let's look at Figure 1 in the activity for an example. If $r = 3$, then $r^2 = 9$. If $OP = 1$, then $OQ = 9$ and point *R* is 4 units to the right of point *P.* That puts the point 2 units outside the circle on segment *PQ.* (See also Activities 21, 27, 28, 33, 35, and 37.)

[9] Inversive geometry deals with the results and the properties of a special transformation called inversion. The inversion of a point *Q* in the circle with center *O* and radius *r* is the unique point *Q′* on the ray *OQ* for which the distance $OQ' = \frac{r^2}{OQ}$. The circle is called the inverting circle or the mirror circle. For an amusing and very readable introduction to inversive geometry, see Marta Sved, *Journey into Geometries,* Chapter 2 (Washington, DC: Mathematical Association of America, 1991). For computer activities about inversion, see James King, *Geometry Through the Circle with The Geometer's Sketchpad* (Berkeley, CA: Key Curriculum Press, 1996).

31 A Two-Piece Jigsaw

Many children play with jigsaw puzzles and often tackle puzzles that have hundreds of pieces. Here is a jigsaw puzzle with only two pieces that many people find difficult to solve, perhaps because it is three-dimensional.

Using the net shown on the left in Figure 1, make two identical models like those shown on the right in Figure 1.

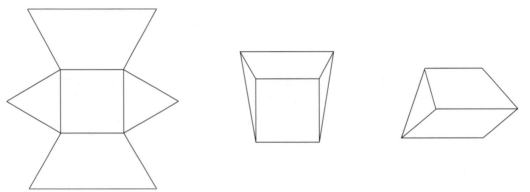

Figure 1

Now fit the two congruent polyhedra together to form a tetrahedron.

Can you do it?

31

A Two-Piece Jigsaw

Explanation

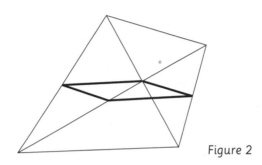

Figure 2

Comments

- Many people have great difficulty solving this puzzle.

- Here is a related problem that students can discuss when they have completed the activity.

Problem:

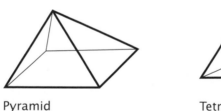

Pyramid   Tetrahedron

Figure 3

In Figure 3, the pyramid has a square base and four faces, each an equilateral triangle. The tetrahedron has four faces, each an equilateral triangle. The edges of the pyramid and of the tetrahedron are of the same length.

Imagine the two solids glued together, with two triangular faces connected edge to edge. How many plane faces do you predict the resulting solid will have? Now, using the nets shown in Figure 4, construct the solids, glue them together, and check the resulting solid. How accurate was your prediction?

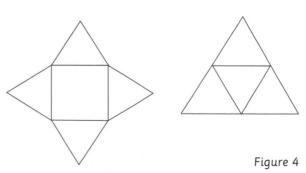

Figure 4

Solution:

The usual prediction is seven (five faces of the pyramid plus four faces of the tetrahedron minus two faces glued together). The correct answer is five! When the two faces are joined, there are two faces in the front (one on the pyramid, one on the tetrahedron) that in fact lie in the same plane and thus combine to form just one plane face. And similarly, at the back there is a pair of faces that come together to form one plane face.

Figure 5

It is not obvious from Figure 5 that the two "front" faces and the two "back" faces will lie in the same plane. Even a demonstration using three-dimensional models may not be convincing enough, though it will add plausibility. A careful proof that there are two pairs of coplanar faces is needed.

Start with a tetrahedron whose side lengths are double the side lengths of the original tetrahedron. Join the midpoints of four edges, as shown in Figure 6.

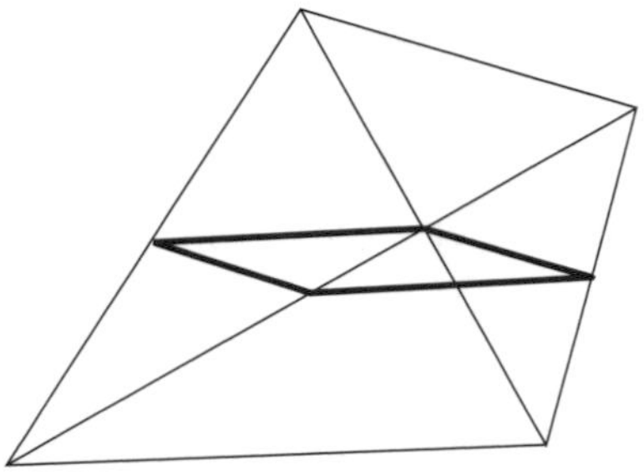

Figure 6

The figure thus formed is a square because its four sides are equal in length and its two diagonals are equal in length. The square divides the tetrahedron into the two congruent polyhedra in the activity. Now draw four more lines from the vertices of the square to the midpoints of a fifth side. This forms a pyramid, *ABCDE,* with a square base and equilateral sides, as shown in Figure 7.

Now it is easy to see that the tetrahedron *ADEF* and the pyramid *ABCDE* are the same as the solids given at the beginning of this problem and that the pairs of faces, *FEA* and *EAB,* and *FED* and *EDC,* are coplanar faces.[10]

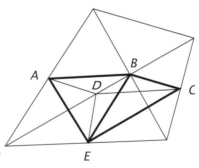

Figure 7

---

[10] An interesting sidelight to this problem is that it was given as Problem 44 in the Preliminary Scholastic Aptitude Test, October 1980, with the *wrong* answer, 7. A seventeen-year-old Florida student, Daniel Lowen, objected when his answer, 5, was marked wrong. He lodged an objection, which was upheld. As a result the scores of nearly 250,000 high school students who took the test were raised.

32 The Surface Area of a Sphere

Textbooks will tell you that the surface area of a sphere with radius r is $4\pi r^2$. Let's develop a different formula: $\pi^2 r^2$. Because $\pi < 4$, this new formula must be wrong. Read the following argument carefully and see whether you can find what is wrong with it.

Divide the equator of a sphere into n equal pieces. If the sphere has radius r, the equator has length $2\pi r$ and each of the equal pieces has length $\frac{2\pi r}{n}$. Draw great circles through the partition points and through the north and south poles.

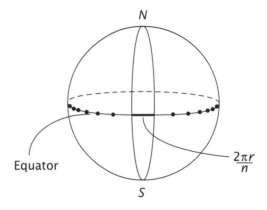

Figure 1

Slice the surface of the sphere along the great circles, peel the slices back, and flatten them out, as shown in Figure 2.

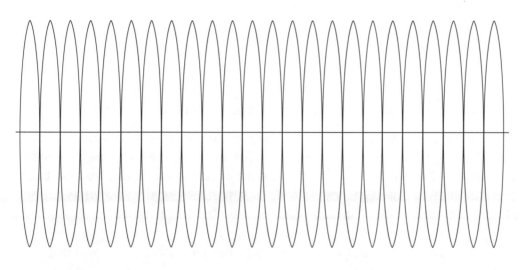

Figure 2

The surface of the sphere has now been flattened out into $2n$ wedges in the shape of isosceles triangles, each with base $\frac{2\pi r}{n}$ and height $\frac{2\pi r}{4}$ (a quarter of the circumference of the sphere). Their total area is $2n \cdot \frac{1}{2} \cdot \frac{2\pi r}{n} \cdot \frac{2\pi r}{4} = \pi^2 r^2$.

How could this be?

This activity was adapted from V. Dubrovsky, "In Search of a Definition of Surface Area," *Quantum* 1, no. 4 (1991).

KEY CONCEPTS
- Area and perimeter of circles
- Area of triangles
- Limits
- Spheres
- Spheres, surface area of
- Spheres, volume of

32

The Surface Area of a Sphere

Explanation

When the sphere is peeled and the slices are flattened out, their area is distorted, resulting in the wrong area formula. The flaw in the argument of this activity is in the action of flattening out the curved slices obtained by cutting through the n great circles and then considering each as a triangle or a circular sector.

The area of a slice is $\frac{n}{360} \cdot \frac{4}{3}\pi r^3$.

There is no way of "flattening" a slice of the surface of a sphere and keeping the measure of its sides unchanged without changing the area.

Comments

- Many arguments in calculus rely on cutting up a surface or a volume into thin slices and then adding the slices together. The incorrect formula in this activity, with its very plausible derivation, shows the need for exercising great care in constructing arguments of this form.

- To help students get a concrete conception of the surface area of a sphere, ask them to cut along the equator of a tennis ball so that they get two hemispheres. Then ask them to place one of the hemispheres on a piece of paper, with the curved part uppermost, and trace around it. Repeat three times to get four circles. These four circles cover the surface area of the ball.

- Though the area of a wedge changes when it is "flattened," because it takes stretching to flatten it without tearing it, other properties may be preserved despite the stretch. Such properties are the focus of the relatively new branch of mathematics called geometric topology, metaphorically known as rubber sheet geometry. This geometry was invented by Henri Poincaré (1854–1912) and deals with those geometric relationships and properties that are preserved by continuous deformations, such as stretching a rubber sheet without tearing it.[11]

---

[11] For some topics in topology at the high school level, see Harold R. Jacobs, *Mathematics: A Human Endeavor: A Textbook for Those Who Think They Don't Like the Subject,* Chapter 10 (San Francisco: W. H. Freeman, 1982).

33 The Lost Square

Cut an 8 × 8 square along the bold lines shown in Figure 1.

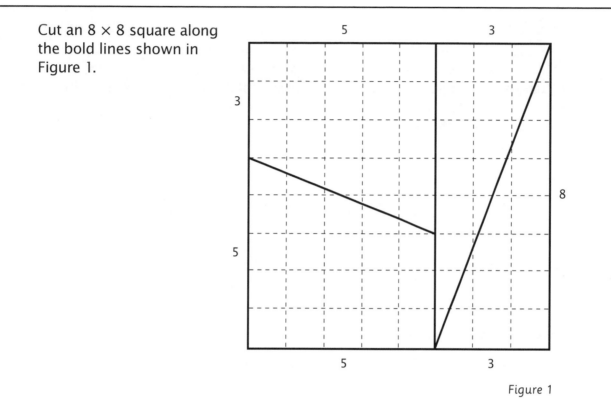

Figure 1

Now rearrange the pieces to form a rectangle, as shown in Figure 2.

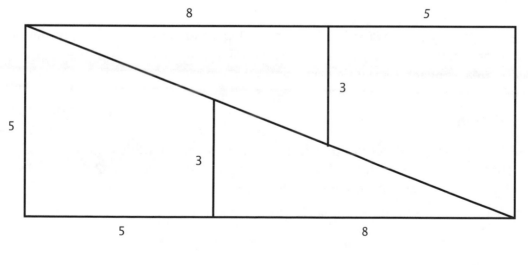

S = 65

Figure 2

The area of the square is 8 × 8 = 64, and the area of the rectangle is 5 × 13 = 65. Where did the extra area in the rectangle come from?

KEY CONCEPTS
- Area equivalence
- Fibonacci sequence
- Relying on figures
- Right-angle triangle trigonometry

33

The Lost Square

Explanation

There is a 1-unit-square difference between the area of the square and the area of the rectangle, which means that the pieces of the square cannot cover the whole rectangle. Indeed they do not. The rearrangement of the pieces may look like Figure 2 in the activity, but in fact the diagonal of the rectangle does not coincide with the sides of the pieces. Figure 3 is a little exaggerated to demonstrate the actual situation.

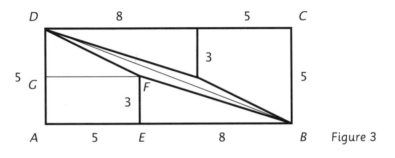

Figure 3

From the figure, we can see that

$$\tan \angle EBF = \frac{3}{8}$$

$$\tan \angle ABD = \frac{5}{13}$$

$$\tan \angle GFD = \frac{2}{5}.$$

Because $\frac{3}{8} < \frac{5}{13} < \frac{2}{5}$, $\angle EBF < \angle ABD < \angle GFD$. Therefore, the pieces do not quite fit together along the diagonal, and between the pieces lies a thin parallelogram with area of exactly 1 square unit.

Comments

- The numbers 5, 8, and 13 that form the basis of this paradox are three successive terms of the well-known Fibonacci sequence, 1, 1, 2, 3, 5, 8, 13, 21, 34, . . . , which is defined as follows:

$$a_1 = a_2 = 1$$

$$a_{(n+1)} = a_n + a_{(n-1)} \text{ for } n \geq 2.$$

Among the many interesting properties of this sequence is the formula $a^2_n - a_{(n-1)} \cdot a_{(n+1)} = -1^{(n-1)}$. In particular, $8^2 - 5 \cdot 13 = -1$ (for $n = 6$).

We can construct a similar dissection paradox using the next triplet of Fibonacci numbers, 8, 13, 21, which gives $13^2 - 8 \cdot 21 = 1$ (see Figure 4).

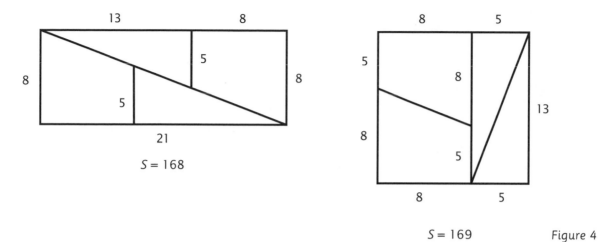

$S = 168$

$S = 169$ Figure 4

In this case the pieces again do not quite fit along the diagonal—they overlap a little.

- This paradox shows that small differences in figures may not be detectable to the eye and that we need to examine geometric "proofs by dissection" carefully. For example, one well-known "proof" that the angles of a triangle add up to 180° depends on cutting up the triangle and rearranging the pieces to fit along a straight line.

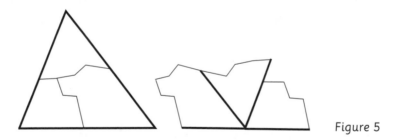

Figure 5

In practice the pieces never fit exactly, and without further argument there is no reason why they should. This "proof" has no better grounds than the "proof" that 64 units^2 = 65 units^2. It therefore has limited mathematical value without further argument.

- Some proofs of the Pythagorean theorem rely on dissection. For example,

$$c^2 = (a - b)^2 + 4 \cdot \frac{1}{2} \cdot ab$$

$$= a^2 - 2ab + b^2 + 2ab$$

$$= a^2 + b^2.$$

We need to examine Figure 6 carefully to ensure that the pieces fit together in exactly the way it suggests.

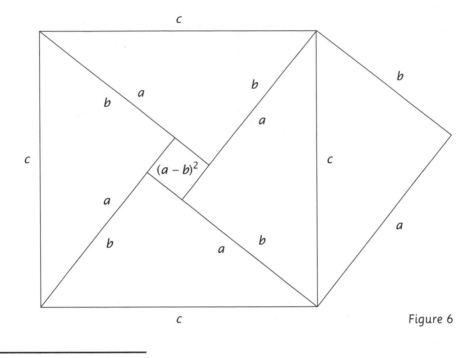

Figure 6

Historical Background

The puzzle in this activity was devised by English mathematician Charles Lutwidge Dodgson (1832–1898), who is better known by his pen name, Lewis Carroll, and for authoring *Alice's Adventures in Wonderland*.[12]

---

[12] For more of Dodgson's puzzles, see Collingwood Stuart Dodgson, ed., *The Unknown Lewis Carroll: Eight Major Works and Many Minor* (Mineola, NY: Dover, 1961). Collingwood Stuart was Charles Lutwidge's nephew and biographer.

---

34 Earth Versus a Ping-Pong™ Ball

1. Imagine a string tied around the equator of a sphere. Untie the string, lengthen it by 1 meter, and form with it a circle concentric with the equator. For the following, estimate intuitively the distance between the new circle and the surface of the sphere:

   a. The sphere is about the size of a Ping-Pong ball.

   b. The sphere is about the size of Earth.

   What is your estimate for each sphere? In the table below, check beside your estimates.

For a Ping-Pong ball	For Earth
___ A few millimeters (less than 1 cm)	___ A few millimeters (less than 1 cm)
___ Between 1 cm and 10 cm	___ Between 1 cm and 10 cm
___ More than 10 cm but less than 0.5 m	___ More than 10 cm but less than 0.5 m
___ Between 0.5 m and 1 m	___ Between 0.5 m and 1 m
___ More than 1 m	___ More than 1 m

2. Now, let's determine mathematically the distance between the surface of any sphere with radius r and a string like that described in part 1 of this activity. What is your result?

3. How do your estimates in part 1 compare with the result you obtained in part 2?

34

Earth Versus a Ping-Pong™ Ball

KEY CONCEPTS
- Circles
- Circumference
- Equators
- Proofs
- Spheres

Explanation

Intuitively, most estimate a long distance for the Ping-Pong ball and a very short distance for Earth. However, the mathematical calculations yield the same distance of $\frac{1}{2\pi}$ for all spheres, independent of their radius.

The circumference of a sphere whose radius is r meters is $2\pi r$, and the circumference of the circle made out of the lengthened string is $2\pi r + 1$. The radius of the circle formed by the lengthened string is $\frac{2\pi r + 1}{2\pi}$. The distance from the surface of the sphere is the difference between the two radii, namely, $\frac{2\pi r + 1}{2\pi} - r = \frac{1}{2\pi}$, which is independent of r.

Comments

- Adding 1 meter to the circumference of a Ping-Pong ball, which measures much less than 1 meter, is a relatively large matter. Adding 1 meter to the circumference of the Earth, which measures about 40,000,000 meters, is negligible.

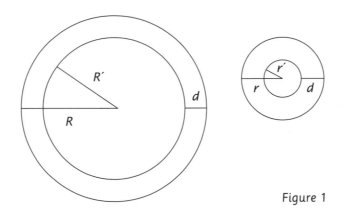

Figure 1

It is therefore very surprising that the distance from the surface of the sphere to the string is the same for the two spheres. Figure 1 shows that $R - R' = r - r' = d$, while the ratio $R : R'$ is less than $2 : 1$ and the ratio $r : r'$ is greater than $2 : 1$.

- A more general lesson can be learned from this activity: Intuition may be very misleading! When we visualize in our minds the situation described in this activity, the relative sizes of the spheres dominate our intuition. We must not trust our mental images blindly. Visual images, even those we can actually look at, can sometimes be very misleading.

35 A Tangram Paradox

The tangram is a well-known puzzle consisting of seven geometrically-shaped pieces: a square, a parallelogram, and five isosceles right triangles (two small, two large, and one medium-sized). The seven pieces fit together to form a square. Their relative sizes are illustrated in Figure 1.

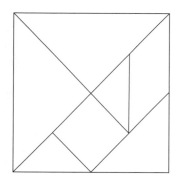

Figure 1

Figures 2, 3, and 4, shown on the following page, show three different ways to construct the shape of a drinking glass from the seven pieces. All three glasses look the same and are made of the same seven pieces. But while all the space of the glass in Figure 2 is filled, the glasses in Figures 3 and 4 are each missing triangular spaces. How could this be?

(Activity 35 is continued on page 98.)

This activity was adapted from Sam Loyd, *The Eighth Book of Tan* (Mineola, NY: Dover, 1968): 25–26.

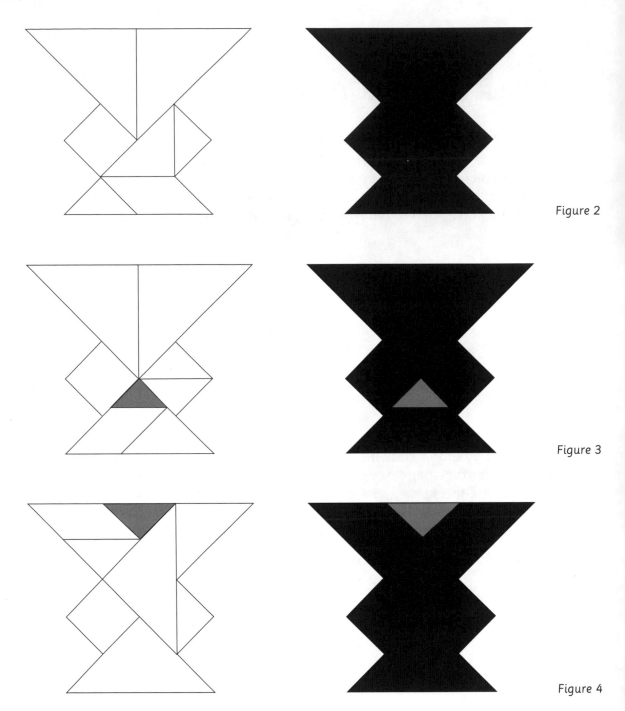

Figure 2

Figure 3

Figure 4

35

A Tangram Paradox

Explanation

The dark area is the same in all the glasses. However, the height of the glasses is not the same, although the glasses look very much alike. The glass in Figure 3 is slightly taller than the glass in Figure 2, and the glass in Figure 4 is slightly wider at the top. These variations make the room for the open spaces.

Comments

- An alternative way to present this paradox is to show Figure 2 and only the blackened shapes in Figures 3 and 4. Ask students whether six pieces will do to construct Figures 3 and 4, as each (seemingly) has the same shape but with small triangular areas removed. The answer is no, of course, because the glasses do *not* have the same shape.

- Here is a similar problem. Compare the two shapes in Figure 5 and observe that although their outside dimensions are equal, the pieces in the second shape are *not* congruent with those of the first shape. The pieces in the second shape are slightly smaller, which makes room for the "missing" corner.

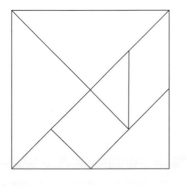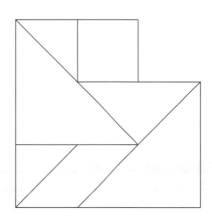

Figure 5

This problem is particularly relevant when your students are studying the equivalent area of polygons. For example, the area of a parallelogram is usually derived from the area of a rectangle by cutting the rectangle into pieces and rearranging them. After rearranging, we must verify that the area is indeed preserved (see also Activity 33).

Historical Background

This Chinese puzzle, known today as a tangram, was a very popular entertainment throughout Asia, Europe, and North America in the nineteenth century. Hundreds of patterns can be created with the seven pieces. French leader Napoleon Bonaparte and American author Edgar Allan Poe were said to be very fond of this puzzle.

The origin of the name *tangram* is very obscure. In China it was known as the Puzzle of the Seven Subtle Shapes. Nineteenth-century amateur mathematician Sam Loyd wrote a book titled *The Eighth Book of Tan* (available from Dover Publications), explaining that thousands of years ago a Chinese man named Tan compiled seven books of patterns created with the seven puzzle pieces. However, a study of Chinese literature and history has revealed no evidence of Tan or of his books, and it is now believed that the story was a figment of Loyd's fertile imagination. Nevertheless, the puzzle has long been popular in China, and in the nineteenth century, sailors who had traveled to China brought the puzzle to Europe and North America.

See Also

See also Activities 21, 27, 28, 30, 33, and 37.

36 The Ratio of Surface Area to Volume

1. The side of the cube in Figure 1 measures d. What is the ratio of the surface area of the cube to its volume?

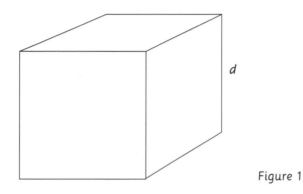

Figure 1

2. The diameter of the sphere in Figure 2 measures d. What is the ratio of the surface area of the sphere to its volume?

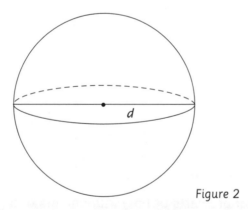

Figure 2

3. Can you come up with any conjecture based on the results you obtained in parts 1 and 2?

4. It is well known that among all solids of equal volume, the sphere is the solid of minimum surface, hence has minimal surface-area-to-volume ratio. But the cube has the same surface-to-volume ratio as the sphere, namely, $\frac{6}{d}$. Does this prove that the cube also has the property of minimal surface-area-to-volume ratio?

This activity was inspired by Christopher P. Jargoski, *Science Brain Twisters, Paradoxes, and Fallacies* (New York: Charles Scribner's, 1976): 3.

- Distorting theorems
- Minima and maxima
- Surface area and volume of solids
- Surface-area-to-volume ratio

36

The Ratio of Surface Area to Volume

Explanation

1. The surface area of the cube is $6d^2$.

   The volume of the cube is d^3.

   The ratio of the surface area to the volume is $\frac{6}{d}$.

2. The surface area of the sphere is πd^2.

   The volume of the sphere is $\frac{\pi d^3}{6}$.

   The ratio of the surface area to the volume is $\frac{6}{d}$.

3. Though the equality of the results is very tempting, there is no basis for any conjecture about the surface-area-to-volume ratio.

4. The results of parts 1 and 2 do *not* contradict the minimality of the surface-area-to-volume ratio for a sphere, because the minimality property holds among solids with the *same* volume. The cube and the sphere described in this activity are not of the same volume; hence it is not surprising that they have the same surface-area-to-volume ratio.

Comments

- Students who recently learned that among all solids of equal volume the sphere has the minimal surface-area-to-volume ratio may fall into the trap in this activity and get confused by the equal results in parts 1 and 2. It is very important for students to realize the significance of the limitation of this principle to solids of equal volume.

- Quite often we ignore parts of the requirements of a principle and apply the principle where it is not applicable. Similar distortions of theorems result in many errors. You may find it very useful to draw students' attention to such a pattern of mistakes. (See also Activity 25, which focuses on omitting an important part of a congruency rule.)[13]

See Also

For more about surface area and volume, see Activities 36, 57, and 58.

[13] For more examples of this type of problem, see N. Movshovitz-Hadar, S. Inbar, and O. Zaslavsky, "Students' Distortions of Theorems," *FOCUS on Learning Problems in Mathematics* 8, no. 1 (1986): 49–57.

37 Pick's Paradox

1. A few simple polygons are shown in Figure 1. For each polygon, the number of interior lattice points (*I*) and the number of boundary points (*B*) are given. Pick's theorem says,

$$\text{Area} = I + \frac{B}{2} - 1.$$

Pick's theorem is a formula for working out the area of a polygon when all its vertices are lattice points (points in the Cartesian plane whose coordinates are integers). All you have to do to find the area of the polygon is count the lattice points inside the polygon and on its boundary.

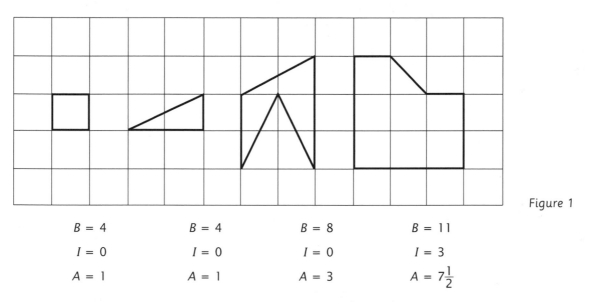

Figure 1

$B = 4$	$B = 4$	$B = 8$	$B = 11$
$I = 0$	$I = 0$	$I = 0$	$I = 3$
$A = 1$	$A = 1$	$A = 3$	$A = 7\frac{1}{2}$

Try using Pick's theorem to find the area of some other polygons. You will soon feel that this remarkably simple area formula must be correct. (The proof of the theorem is not obvious but worth an attempt.)

2. Figure 2 seems to suggest that something is wrong: The triangle has base
   length 8 and height 5, so its area is 20. But it contains 14 interior points
   and 15 boundary points, so according to Pick's theorem, its area is $20\frac{1}{2}$.

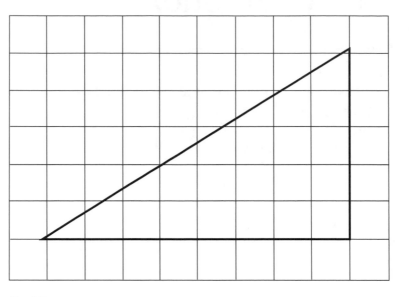

Figure 2

$B = 15$

$I = 14$

$\frac{1}{2} B + I - 1 = \frac{15}{2} + 14 - 1 = 20\frac{1}{2}$

But $\frac{1}{2}$ base $\times$ height $= \frac{1}{2} \times 8 \times 5 = 20$.

What is wrong here?

     One Equals Zero and Other Mathematical Surprises ©1998 by Key Curriculum Press

Pick's Paradox

KEY CONCEPTS
- Area of polygons
- Geometry, coordinate
- Polygons
- Relying on figures

Explanation

1. Pick's theorem can easily be verified for a rectangle whose sides are *m* and *n* units in length. There is more than one way to prove Pick's theorem. See the fourth comment in this activity for one way.

2. Assuming the origin of the coordinates is at the lower-left hand vertex of the triangle, the other two vertices have coordinates (8, 0) and (8, 5). The slope of the hypotenuse is $\frac{5}{8}$, and because $\frac{2}{3} > \frac{5}{8}$, the point (3, 2) lies above the hypotenuse, that is, outside the triangle. Thus, there are 14 boundary points, not 15. With this correction, Pick's theorem gives the right area.

Comments

- Pick's theorem is nicely exhibited on a geoboard. Using rubber bands to form polygons, students should be able to verify Pick's theorem for as many different polygons as they wish.

- The paradox in part 2 of this activity is really an optical illusion. Encourage students to use their geoboards to experience it. Because the fractions $\frac{2}{3}$ and $\frac{5}{8}$ are quite close in value, the eye cannot readily detect the difference in slope of the two parts of the hypotenuse. Thus the eye is deceived into thinking that the point (3, 2) lies on the hypotenuse. (See also Activity 33.)

- You can devise more examples that seem to contradict Pick's theorem, using pairs of fractions whose values are very close to each other, such as $\frac{3}{5}$ and $\frac{5}{8}$. In fact, any three successive terms of the Fibonacci sequence, 1, 1, 2, 3, 5, 8, 13, 21, . . . , will give such pairs: $\frac{2}{3}$ and $\frac{3}{5}$, $\frac{3}{5}$ and $\frac{5}{8}$, $\frac{5}{8}$ and $\frac{8}{13}$, and so on.

- Pick's theorem deserves a proof.

  Consider any polygon *P* that has *B* boundary lattice points and *I* interior lattice points.

  P can be dissected into triangles any number of different ways. We shall call a triangle with no interior lattice point and just three boundary points a *fundamental triangle*. For our proof, we dissect *P* into fundamental triangles, which also can be done in many different ways.

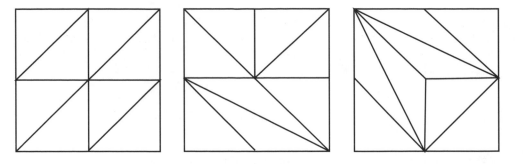

Figure 3

In step 1 below, we show first that the number of fundamental triangles in every dissection of P is the same and is in fact $2I + B - 2$. In step 2 we show that the area of each fundamental triangle is $\frac{1}{2}$. Together, these two facts imply that the area of P is $I + \frac{B}{2} - 1$.

1. To show that the number of fundamental triangles in every dissection of P is the same, suppose the polygon is dissected into m fundamental triangles, as shown in Figure 4. Let the number of boundary points be B and the number of interior points be I.

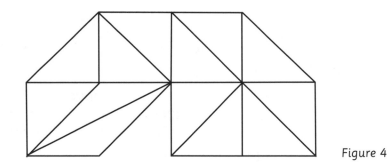

Figure 4

Now add up all the angles in the figure in two different ways: Each triangle has an angle sum of 180°, so the sum of all the angles is $m \cdot 180°$. On the other hand, the sum of all the inside angles is $I \cdot 360°$ because around each interior point we have an angle sum of 360°. Because the polygon has B vertices, it can be dissected into $B - 2$ triangles and the sum of its angles is $(B - 2) \cdot 180°$.

Therefore,

$$m \cdot 180° = I \cdot 360° + (B - 2) \cdot 180°,$$

which gives

$$m = 2I + B - 2,$$

and this is true for every dissection. This completes the proof of step 1.

2. It now remains to show that the area of any fundamental triangle is $\frac{1}{2}$.

Let T be any triangle with one vertex at the origin. If the coordinates of the three vertices of the triangle are $(0, 0)$, (a, b), and (c, d), then the area of T

is $\frac{1}{2}(|ad - bc|)$. In particular, if the vertices are lattice points (so a, b, c, and d are integers), the area of T is at least $\frac{1}{2}$. This is also true for triangles with vertices at lattice points other than the origin.

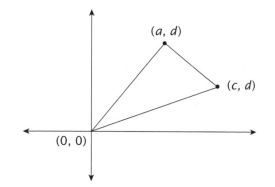

Figure 5

If T is a fundamental triangle, it may be enclosed by an $m \times n$ rectangle R. This rectangle may then be dissected into fundamental triangles, one of which is T, as illustrated in Figure 6 (with $m = 3$ and $n = 2$).

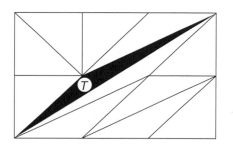

Figure 6

On the other hand, the $m \times n$ rectangle can be dissected into $2mn$ congruent fundamental triangles, as shown in Figure 7.

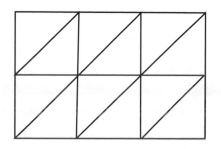

Figure 7

We therefore have:

$$mn = \text{area } (R) = \text{area } (T) + \text{area (other triangles)}$$
$$\geq 2mn \cdot \frac{1}{2} = mn.$$

So the area of $T = \frac{1}{2}$.

That completes the proof of step 2.

With these two facts established to get the area of P, we dissect P into $2I + B - 2$ fundamental triangles, each of area $\frac{1}{2}$, which implies

$$\text{Area } (P) = (2I + B - 2) \cdot \frac{1}{2} = I + \frac{B}{2} - 1. \text{ Q.E.D.}$$

Historical Background

Very little is known about Austrian mathematician Georg Pick (1859–1943). He published his theorem in 1899, and in 1911 he worked with Albert Einstein (1879–1955). Pick died in Therezienstadt concentration camp.

38 Which Strip Has the Greatest Area?

In Figure 1, four strips of width *d* are marked 1, 2, 3, and 4. The strips connect the two parallel lines *PP′* and *QQ′*.

Which strip has the greatest area?

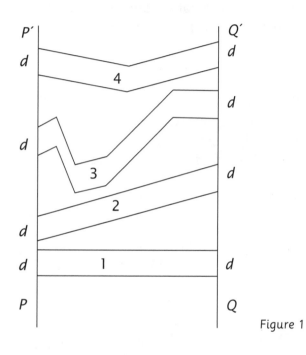

Figure 1

KEY CONCEPTS
- Area between parallel lines
- Area equivalence
- Area of rectangles
- Area of parallelograms
- Cavalieri's principle
- Volume

38

Which Strip Has the Greatest Area?

Explanation

All four strips have the same area. This may not look true, but we can easily verify it.

To show that rectangle 1 and parallelogram 2 have the same area, simply draw the rectangle in such a way that its vertices coincide with the vertices of the parallelogram, as shown in Figure 2. Now consider the area of parallelogram *ABEF* as the difference between the areas of trapezoid *ABCF* and triangle *BCE*. Because triangles *BCE* and *ADF* are congruent, they have the same area. Therefore, the area of the parallelogram is also the difference between the areas of trapezoid *ABCF* and triangle *ADF*, which is exactly the area of rectangle *ABCD*.

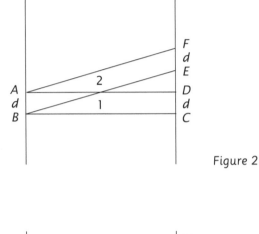

Figure 2

Observe in Figure 3 that the area of polygon 3 is the difference between the areas of polygon *EFGHIJCB* and polygon *E'F'G'H'I'J'CB*. The area of polygon *E'F'G'H'I'J'CB* equals the area of polygon *EFGHIJDA* because the two are congruent. Thus, the area of polygon 3 is exactly the same as the difference between the areas of polygon *EFGHIJCB* and polygon *EFGHIJDA*, which is the area of rectangle *ABCD*.

Using similar reasoning, it is easy to observe that polygon 4 has the same area as the other strips.

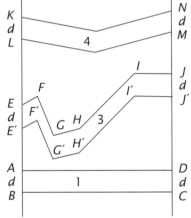

Figure 3

Comments

- Similarly, the area of any strip of width *d* that connects the two parallel lines is also the same as the area of rectangle 1—even a wiggly strip!

- A common mistake is to say that rectangle 1 has the least area. It is indeed the strip with the shortest side (the side that is not of length *d*, of course), but that does not make it least in area. This illusion might be caused by the side of length *d* that is common to all the shapes. However, note that only in rectangle 1 is *d* also the distance between the other two (parallel) sides. Because the distance is the shortest segment, it is the perpendicular to the two (parallel) sides of the strip and it is *not* of length *d* in the other strips. Figure 4 illustrates the difference.

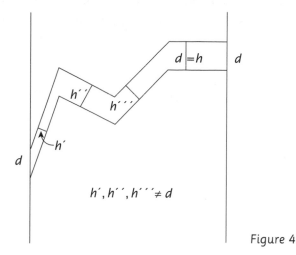

$$h', h'', h''' \neq d$$

Figure 4

- Let's look at the meaning of *parallel curves*. The intuitive interpretation is that two lines are parallel if the shortest distance between them is constant. Another interpretation is that two curves are parallel if one is a displacement, or translation, of the other. The lines in strip 3 are parallel in the second sense but not in the first. The two notions of parallel curves coincide when the curves are straight lines but not otherwise, as seen in Figure 5.

- This activity emphasizes a very useful principle: The area of a strip created between two (straight) parallel lines by two (possibly broken or curved) line displacements depends only upon *d*, the measure of the line displacement creating the strip, and the distance between the two parallel lines, *not* upon the shape of the two (possibly curved or broken) lines that connect them.

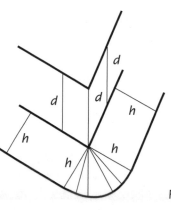

Figure 5

Thus, there is no need to know integral calculus to determine the area of a strip between two identical curves. This is a particular case of Cavalieri's principle: If two planar pieces are included between a pair of parallel lines, and if the lengths of the two segments cut by them on any line parallel to the including lines are in the same ratio, then the areas of the two planar pieces are also in this ratio.

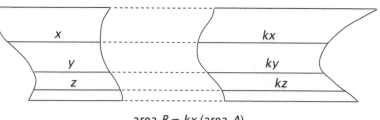

area $B = kx$ (area A)

Figure 6

- There is a three-dimensional analog of Cavalieri's principle. If two solids are of equal height and have bases with areas in the ratio $a : b$, and if all plane sections parallel to the bases and at the same distance from the corresponding bases have areas in the ratio $a : b$, then the two solids have volumes in the ratio $a : b$. You can demonstrate this principle in class with a stack of cards.

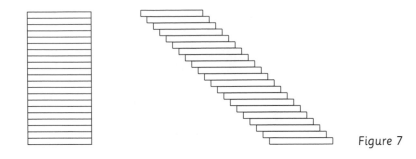

Figure 7

Historical Background

Italian mathematics professor Bonaventura Cavalieri (1598–1647) was a student of Galileo Galilei (1564–1642). In his book *Geometria Indivisibilibus Continuorum* (1635), Cavalieri put forward the notion of an "indivisible" as a sort of "atomic part" of a plane or solid figure. According to Cavalieri, an indivisible of a plane curve is an infinitely small chord. He regarded a plane figure as being made of infinitely many indivisibles, or infinitely small parallel cuts, and a solid as being made of infinitely many parallel plane sections, each infinitely thin. Cavalieri's principle enabled mathematicians to determine the area of plane figures (respectively, the volume of solids) whose boundaries are curved lines (respectively, curved surfaces). His methods were early forerunners of the contemporary techniques of integral calculus.

39 The Average Math Score Paradox

Pátria and Bruce were discussing their math test results. "I took 6 tests in the first semester and passed 5 of them," said Pátria.

"That is better than my performance," said Bruce. "I passed only 8 out of the 10 tests I took, and $\frac{5}{6} > \frac{8}{10}$. How did you do in the second semester, Pátria?"

"Not so well as in the first semester. I took 14 tests, but passed only 6."

"I did not do so well in the second semester either," said Bruce. "I managed to pass only 4 out of 10, but you still did better than I did, because $\frac{6}{14} > \frac{4}{10}$."

"Just wait a minute, Pátria," said Bruce. "You did better than I did in both semesters, but we both took 20 tests, right?"

"Sure!" agreed Pátria.

"Well, I passed 12 altogether, 8 in the first semester and 4 in the second, and you passed only 11, 5 in the first and 6 in the second. That means I did better than you over the two semesters."

"Hey, that does not add up!" said Pátria indignantly. "If I did better than you in each of the two semesters separately, how could you have done better than I did overall? Let's check those figures again."

And they did, but the numbers came out just the same. How would you help Pátria and Bruce sort out this paradox?

KEY CONCEPTS
- Averages
- Fractions
- Inequalities

39

The Average Math Score Paradox

Explanation

This paradox highlights the danger of placing too much faith in an average. An average is a figure taken out of a bunch of data in an attempt to highlight some specific character of the data. Taking an average always means losing information. Therefore, comparing averages may not always reflect a full picture. Pátria and Bruce had taken different numbers of tests in the two semesters, and they compared their performances by looking at their pass rates. When they compared their overall performance, they expected the order of their respective yearly pass rates to be consistent with that of the two semester pass rates, but rates may not behave this way.

Comments

- A probability version of this paradox can be played in the classroom. Begin with two boxes marked A and B. In box A put 5 white balls and 1 red ball (or 5 white pieces of chalk and 1 colored piece). In box B put 8 white balls and 2 red balls. Invite a student to select a box and draw a ball at random from that box. If the student knows how many balls of each color are in each box, which box should she or he select to ensure the better chance of drawing a white ball?

Because the chance of drawing a white ball from box A is $\frac{5}{6}$ and the chance of drawing a white ball from box B is $\frac{8}{10}$, and $\frac{5}{6} > \frac{8}{10}$, it is better to select box A. (You may want to record this fact on the blackboard for later reference.)

Now introduce boxes C and D. In box C put 6 white balls and 8 red balls, and in box D put 4 white balls and 6 red balls. Then play the game again. This time the chance of drawing a white ball from box C is $\frac{6}{14}$ and the chance of drawing a white ball from box D is $\frac{4}{10}$. Because $\frac{6}{14} > \frac{4}{10}$, box C provides a better chance of drawing a white ball than box D. (You may want to add this to the previous record on the blackboard and summarize as follows.)

A is better than B, and C is better than D.

Now, add the balls in box C to the balls in box A, thus combining the two boxes that provide a better chance to draw a white ball. Add the balls in box D to the balls in box B. Now there are 20 balls in box A and 20 balls in box B. Ask your students to select the box that provides a better chance of drawing a white ball. For many students the intuitively obvious choice would be box A again. But the calculations give $\frac{11}{20} < \frac{12}{20}$. Discuss the grounds for their incorrect intuitive selection.

- Two interesting, but not easy, investigations are related to this activity.

  1. Find sets of numbers that behave as the numbers in this activity did, namely, a, b, c, d, p, q, r, and s, such that $\frac{a}{b} > \frac{p}{q}$, and $\frac{c}{d} > \frac{r}{s}$, but $\frac{a+c}{b+d} < \frac{p+r}{q+s}$.

  2. For which numbers is the "natural addition rule of fractions" true? That is, for which values of a, b, c, and d do we have $\frac{a}{b} + \frac{c}{d} = \frac{a+c}{b+d}$? One possible answer is $a = 4$, $b = 2$, $c = -9$, and $d = 3$. Can you find others?

- It is rather natural to assume that semester rates will add up as the two semesters add up to the full year, but the logic of averaging is in conflict with intuition here. Of course, this conflict does not mean that intuition must be altogether dismissed. It only means that intuition must be very carefully supported by mathematical arguments.

See Also

For more on the behavior of averages, see Activities 40, 41, 42, and 43.[14]

Historical Background

This paradox is a simple version of a paradox known among statisticians as Simpson's paradox. According to Wagner,[15] Simpson's paradox was discussed in print as early as 1903 by Scottish statistician George Udny Yule.[16] The paradox is named after English statistician E. H. Simpson, who discussed it extensively in his 1951 paper.[17]

---

[14] For further reading about statistical paradoxes, see H. E. Reinhardt, "Some Statistical Paradoxes," *Teaching Statistics and Probability* (1981 Yearbook), ed. A. P. Shuttle and J. R. Smart (Reston, VA: National Council of Teachers of Mathematics, 1981): 100–109.

[15] Clifford H. Wagner, *Simpson's Paradox,* UMAP: Modules and Monographs in Undergraduate Mathematics and its Applications Project, Unit 587 (Newton, MA: EDC/UMAP, 1983).

[16] George U. Yule, "Notes on the Theory of Association of Attributes in Statistics," *Biometrika* 2 (1903): 121–134. Reprinted in *Statistical Papers of George Udny Yule,* comp. A. Stuart and M. G. Kendall (New York: Hafner Publishing, 1971).

[17] E. H. Simpson, "The Interpretation of Interaction in Contingency Tables," *Journal of the Royal Statistical Society, Series B* 13 (1951): 238–241.

40 Whose Average?

At State University a large calculus class of 500 students is divided into three lecture classes of 100 students and one lecture class of 200 students. Four professors are assigned to give the calculus lectures. From the professors' point of view, the average class size is therefore $\frac{500}{4} = 125$.

There is another point of view: that of the students. If you ask the students how many are in their calculus classes, 200 will answer 200 and 300 will answer 100. The average of their answers is $\frac{200 \cdot 200 + 300 \cdot 100}{200 + 300} = 140$.

Which average is correct?

40

Whose Average?

Explanation

Both averages are correct. They reflect two different points of view. The average class size as seen by a professor is 125, and the average class size as seen by the students is 140. Because the points of view are different, the data about class size also differ, and therefore the information conveyed by the average is also different.

Comment

It is interesting to note that in this sort of situation the average perceived by the students is always higher than the average perceived by the professors. A big class is seen by only one professor but is observed by each student in the class and so gets a heavier weight when the average is calculated. We can check this observation algebraically:

If there are n classes with $a_1, a_2, \ldots, a_n$ students, the average class size from the professors' viewpoint is

$$\frac{a_1 + a_2 + \ldots + a_n}{n}.$$

The average class size from the students' viewpoint is

$$\frac{(a_1)^2 + (a_2)^2 + \ldots + (a_n)^2}{a_1 + a_2 + \ldots + a_n}.$$

Now, $n \cdot \sum_{i=1}^{n} (a_i)^2 - \left(\sum_{i=1}^{n} a_i\right)^2 = \sum_{i \neq j}(a_i - a_j)^2 \geq 0$. So $n \cdot \sum_{i=1}^{n} (a_i)^2 \geq \left(\sum_{i=1}^{n} a_i\right)^2$.

In other words,

$$n[(a_1)^2 + (a_2)^2 + \ldots + (a_n)^2] \geq (a_1 + a_2 + \ldots + a_n)(a_1 + a_2 + \ldots + a_n).$$

Hence, $\dfrac{(a_1)^2 + (a_2)^2 + \ldots + (a_n)^2}{a_1 + a_2 + \ldots + a_n} \geq \dfrac{a_1 + a_2 + \ldots + a_n}{n}.$

(This is a special case of Chebyshev's inequality.)

See Also

This activity and Activity 39 deal with the notion of the average representing data. Many peculiarities are related to this notion. For a few more examples, see Activities 41, 42, and 43.

Historical Background

This activity is a simplified version of a paradoxical situation related to the expected value of class sizes at the Harvard School of Public Health, described by Hemenway.[18] The school offered many small classes, but the majority of the students got into large classes. Thus, in Hemenway's example, the average class size was 14.5 but the expected class size for a student was 78.

Nineteenth-century Russian mathematician Pafnuti Lvovich Chebyshev (1821–1894), whose inequality is used in the comment in this activity, made outstanding contributions to probability theory, the theory of integration, and the analytic theory of numbers. One of his many achievements was showing that if $n > 3$, there always exists at least one prime number between n and $2n$. (For more about Chebyshev, see the historical background in Activity 16.)

---

[18] David Hemenway, "Why Your Classes Are Larger Than Average," *Mathematics Magazine* 55 (1982): 162–164.

41 Increasing the Average

In Martin Luther King Jr. School the average IQ of the first-graders is 115. Rosa has an IQ of 110 and is in the first grade of Martin Luther King Jr. School. Her family moves out of the school district, and Rosa enrolls at Jefferson School, where the average IQ of the first-graders is 105.

When Rosa leaves the first grade of Martin Luther King Jr. School, the average IQ of that class rises a little because Rosa's IQ was below the class average. When Rosa enrolls at Jefferson School, the average IQ of her new first-grade class also rises because Rosa's IQ is above the class average.

Is moving Rosa a way to increase the intelligence of the first-graders of the two schools?

41

Increasing the Average

Explanation

Rosa's move did not change her IQ, and it did not change the overall average IQ of the first-graders at the two schools taken together. The two averages of the separate classes increased, but only because that is the way averages can behave. Averages tell the truth and nothing but the truth—but they may not tell the whole truth. And sometimes the truth they tell is not very useful.

See Also

For more on the behavior of averages, see Activities 39, 40, 42, and 43.

42 Almost Everybody Is Above Average

The average height of the adult male population of the United States is 5'9". This figure is also a median: half the men are above this height, and half are below it.

1. Can you think of a physical feature for which almost everybody is above average?

2. Can you think of a measure according to which everybody is exactly average?

42

Almost Everybody Is Above Average

Explanation

1. Count your fingers. The vast majority of people have ten. Some people have lost one or more fingers, but the number of people with more than ten fingers is very low. So, we can conclude that the average number of fingers is a little less than ten. Thus, most people have an above-average number of fingers.

2. Every living person has exactly one head, which is no more, no less than average.

See Also

For more on the behavior of averages, see Activities 39, 40, 41, and 43.

43 Half the World Is Stupid?

A headline of a tabloid newspaper article reads, "Half the World Is Stupid!" The article begins with the statement, "As much as 50% of the world's population has a below-average IQ score!"

Do you find this statement disturbing? Why?

43

Half the World Is Stupid?

Explanation

The statement is true and should not be regarded as disturbing. According to convention, the average IQ score is 100. This measurement of 100 is the average in two senses. Not only is it an *arithmetic mean,* obtained by adding up all individual IQ scores and dividing the sum by the number of people tested, but it is a also a *median,* separating the population into two equal halves. Thus, it is quite true that half the population has a below average IQ score and half the population has an above average IQ score. This example of what *average* means is valid in this, and in many other, contexts.

Researchers and scholars continue to debate what IQ scores really mean, and for that matter, what "intelligence" is. The fact that a certain psychological measurement is labeled an intelligence quotient does not necessarily mean it is a measurement of intelligence in every sense of the word. Additionally, it does not follow that if a person's IQ measurement is below 100, then he or she is "stupid." Even if we accept (and some don't) that an IQ score is an accurate measurement of some human quality, we must recognize that it is a measurement from which sociopolitical conclusions should be drawn with considerable reservations.

Comment

The use of the phrase "as much as" in the statement "As much as 50% of the world's population has a below-average IQ score" is intended to grab the reader's attention. Similar phrases are frequently used in advertising:

Prices from as little as $199.00.

Discounts of as much as 20% offered.

Cut your heating bills by up to 10%.

These statements are far more effective than the following:

Everything costs at least $199.00.

Discounts of more than 20% are not offered.

Your heating bill will not be cut by more than 10%.

Ask students to collect similar examples and bring them to class for discussion.

See Also

For more on the behavior of averages, see Activities 39, 40, 41, and 42.

44 A Chess Tournament Paradox

Three chess teams compete in a triangular tournament. Each team consists of three players. Let's label the players with their rankings from highest (1) to lowest (9): 1, 2, 3, 4, 5, 6, 7, 8, and 9. (The players are very consistent; they never lose to a player below them in rank.)

Team A consists of players 2, 4, and 9.

Team B consists of players 3, 5, and 7.

Team C consists of players 1, 6, and 8.

The teams seem to be equally strong because the average rank of each team is 5.

In the first tournament, the teams rank themselves according to their ability and each player plays one match against his or her opposite number. Thus, when Team A meets Team B,

   2 plays 3,

   4 plays 5, and

   9 plays 7,

   and Team A beats Team B by 2 games to 1.

   When Team B plays Team C,

   3 plays 1,

   5 plays 6, and

   7 plays 8,

and Team B beats Team C by 2 games to 1.

Thus, Team A beats Team B, and Team B beats Team C.

What do you expect will happen when Team C plays Team A? Well, Team C beats Team A by 2 games to 1. This result is rather unexpected. One would tend to believe that if Team A beats Team B and Team B beats Team C, then Team A would beat Team C, not the other way around.

The tournament organizers decide that the tournament has a very unsatisfactory outcome when no clear winner emerges, so they change the rules of the tournament. In the new system, when two teams meet, each team member will play a game against every member of the opposing team.

Let's see what happens when Team A meets Team B. Of the 9 games played, Team A wins 5 (2 beats 3, 5, and 7; and 4 beats 5 and 7), so Team A wins.

When Team B plays Team C, Team B wins 5 games (3 and 5 each beat 6 and 8, and 7 beats 8). Thus, Team B wins.

What will happen when Team C plays Team A? You guessed it! Team C wins 5 games (1 beats 2, 4, and 9; and 6 and 8 both beat 9), so Team C wins.

The tournament organizers are in despair. It seems logical to them that if Team A is better than Team B, and Team B is better than Team C, then surely Team A must be better than Team C! Isn't that what "better than" should mean?

KEY CONCEPTS
- Magic squares
- Order relations
- Transitivity

44

A Chess Tournament Paradox

Explanation

The tournament paradox is an example of a system of ordering in which transitivity does not hold. When we compare numbers, a basic property of inequalities known as transitivity says that if $a > b$ and $b > c$, then $a > c$.

The ordering of real numbers is reflected by the positions of numbers on the number line, as shown in Figure 1.

Figure 1

Thus, $a > b$ because a lies to the right of b on the number line. If a is to the right of b and b is to the right of c, then a is to the right of c.

The ranking of people's heights is another example of an ordering system in which the transitivity property is observed. If we know that Eli is taller than Zack, and Zack is taller than Selena, then Eli is taller than Selena.

The transitivity property allows the lining up of enumerated items. Many common systems of order are transitive but not all. The tournament paradox is a nice example of a system of ordering in which transitivity does not hold.

Comment

Here is an interesting little sidelight on the tournament problem. If the chess teams are arranged as shown below, the numbers make up a 3×3 magic square, in which the rows, columns, and main diagonals sum to the same total.

3×3 magic square (sum 15)

A	B	C
4	3	8
9	5	1
2	7	6

It is interesting to devise a similar paradox, using a 5×5 magic square, that involves a tournament with five teams of five players each. Ask students to try it with the following 5×5 magic square:

5 × 5 magic square (sum 65)

9	2	25	18	11
3	21	19	12	10
22	20	13	6	4
16	14	7	5	23
15	8	1	24	17

Now let students try to devise a similar paradox for four teams, using the magic square below:

4 × 4 magic square (sum 34)

16	3	2	13
5	10	11	8
9	6	7	12
4	15	14	1

(In this case, any two teams draw 2:2. This magic square does not produce a similar paradox.)

_____

See Also

For a related paradox about transitivity, see Activity 45.

45 The Dice Paradox

Suppose you and an opponent play dice. You each roll a conventional fair die, and the player rolling the larger number wins. This is a fair game because each of you has the same chance of winning.

Now look at the unusual dice shown in Figure 1.

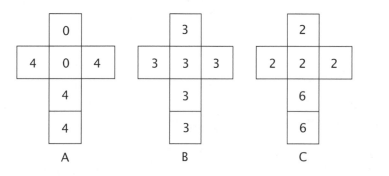

Figure 1

You now play a different game. First you choose a die, then your opponent chooses one of the two remaining dice. You roll your dice at the same time, and the player rolling the larger number wins.

1. If you choose die A and your opponent chooses die B, who will win on average?

2. If you choose die B and your opponent chooses die C, who will win on average?

3. From questions 1 and 2 we can see that, on the balance of probabilities, A beats B, and B beats C. This suggests that when A and C are rolled together, A will beat C. Is that correct? Can you explain what happens?

4. Is it better to choose first or second?

5. If you play first, which of the three dice should you choose to give you the best chance of winning?

6. What happens when the three dice are thrown simultaneously? The average score shown by A is $\frac{8}{3}$, which equals $\frac{1}{6}(0 + 0 + 4 + 4 + 4 + 4)$. The average score shown by B is 3, and the average score shown by C is $\frac{10}{3}$, which equals $\frac{1}{6}(2 + 2 + 2 + 2 + 6 + 6)$. Does this mean that on average the die most likely to win is C, followed by B, then by A?

45

The Dice Paradox

Explanation

1. Let's examine what happens when dice A and B are rolled together. Four times out of six, A's 4 beats B's 3. So the probability that A beats B is $\frac{2}{3}$ and, of course, the probability that B beats A is $\frac{1}{3}$.

2. What happens when B and C are rolled together? Four times out of six, B's 3 beats C's 2. Thus, the probability that B beats C is $\frac{2}{3}$ and the probability that C beats B is $\frac{1}{3}$.

3. When A and C are rolled together, A will win if A shows 4 and B shows 2. The probability that A shows 4 is $\frac{2}{3}$, and the probability that C shows 2 is $\frac{2}{3}$. So the probability that A beats C is $\frac{2}{3} \cdot \frac{2}{3} = \frac{4}{9}$, and thus the probability that C beats A is $\frac{5}{9}$. Therefore, on average, C beats A.

4. It is always better to choose your die second. Whichever die the first player chooses, the second player can choose a die that will beat it.

5. If you have to choose first, you should choose die A because, although it is beaten by C, the probability that it loses to C is $\frac{4}{9}$, which is less than $\frac{2}{3}$ (the probability that B loses to A or that C loses to B).

6. The "average score" argument gives the wrong answer. If the three dice are rolled together,

   A wins when it shows 4 and C shows 2 (probability $\frac{2}{3} \cdot \frac{2}{3} = \frac{4}{9}$),

   B wins when A shows 2 and C shows 2 (probability $\frac{1}{3} \cdot \frac{2}{3} = \frac{2}{9}$), and

   C wins when it shows 6 (probability $\frac{1}{3}$).

Therefore, in a three-way contest, the die most likely to win is A.

Comments

- The argument that the die with highest average face value has the best chance of winning is faulty. The numbers on the faces of the dice could be altered without affecting their chances of winning. For example, if the 0s were changed to 1s on A and the 6s to 5s on C, the average face value of each die would be 3 but their chances of winning would be the same as before.

- You can implement this activity in the classroom by asking students to form groups of three and then letting each group construct one of the three dice. (They can use regular dice, affixing stickers that display the numbers of the dice shown in the activity.) Then have students play the dice game repeatedly

---

and record the results. Students will naturally think of their strategy while playing. Once the activity is completed, the class, guided by you, can formally analyze the dice game—the results will surprise everyone.

- The relative strength of the three dice (A is better than B, B is better than C, and C is better than A) is an example of a nontransitive ordering. (See also Activity 44.)

A transitive order relation R is one in which aRb and bRc implies aRc. An example of such a relation is the usual ordering of the integers, for which $a > b$ and $b > c$ implies that $a > c$ for any three integers a, b, and c. Not all relations that look as if they are transitive are indeed transitive. In this activity, the particular case of the dice beating one another looks at first glance to be transitive, but it is not: A beats B, and B beats C, yet A does not beat C. This circularity is what makes the role of the first player really tough. No matter what the first player plays, the second can pick a die that has a better chance of winning.

Historical Background

A set of four "nontransitive dice" were invented by Bradley Efron (b 1938), Professor of Statistics and Biostatistics at Stanford University, California. Efron is also a Max H. Stein Professor of Humanities and Sciences. Three of his dice were used in this activity. His fourth die is D: 5, 5, 5, 1, 1, 1.

46 The Random Chord Paradox

A chord is drawn at random in a circle of radius 1. What is the probability that the length of the chord will be $\sqrt{3}$ or more? Let's look at three different solution methods for this problem.

Method 1:

Fix a point P on the circumference of the circle and draw a chord PQ at an angle θ to the tangent at point P, where θ is chosen at random between 0° and 180° (see Figure 1).

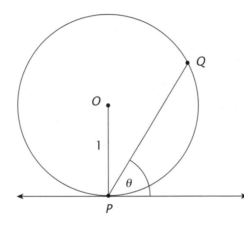

Figure 1

For which angles θ is the length of chord PQ $\sqrt{3}$ or more? What is the probability that a chord drawn at random in this way will have length $\sqrt{3}$ or more?

Method 2:

Choose a point M at a random distance r from the center O of the circle, and draw a chord with midpoint M perpendicular to segment OM (see Figure 2). Here r is chosen at random between 0 and 1.

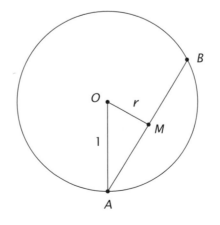

Figure 2

For which values of *r* is the length of chord *AB* $\sqrt{3}$ or more? What is the probability that a chord drawn at random in this way will have length $\sqrt{3}$ or more?

Method 3:

Choose a random point *N*(*x, y*) inside the circle with center *O*(0, 0). Through point *N* draw a chord *CD* perpendicular to segment *ON*.

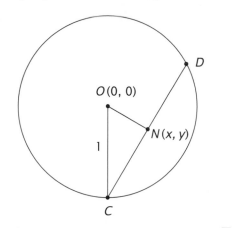

Figure 3

For which values of *x* and *y* is the length of chord *CD* $\sqrt{3}$ or more? What is the probability that a chord drawn at random in this way will have length $\sqrt{3}$ or more?

Compare the probabilities you obtained by using the three different methods. Which (if any) is the correct answer to our question?

46

The Random Chord Paradox

Explanation

Method 1 (see Figure 4):

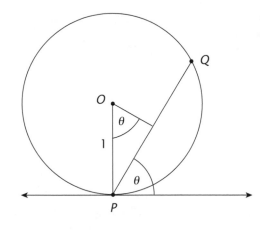

Figure 4

$$PQ = 2 \sin \theta.$$

Therefore,

$$PQ \geq \sqrt{3}$$

$$\Leftrightarrow \quad 2 \sin \theta \geq \sqrt{3}$$

$$\Leftrightarrow \quad \sin \theta \geq \frac{\sqrt{3}}{2}$$

$$\Leftrightarrow \quad 60° \leq \theta \leq 120°.$$

Thus, the required probability is $\dfrac{120 - 60}{180} = \dfrac{1}{3}$.

Method 2 (see Figure 5):

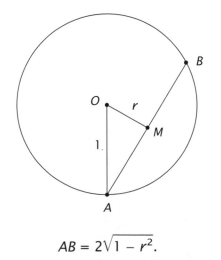

Figure 5

$$AB = 2\sqrt{1 - r^2}.$$

Therefore,

$$AB \geq \sqrt{3}$$

$$\Leftrightarrow \quad (1 - r^2) \geq \frac{3}{4}$$

$$\Leftrightarrow \quad r^2 \leq \frac{1}{4}$$

$$\Leftrightarrow \quad 0 \leq r \leq \frac{1}{2} \text{ (because } r \geq 0).$$

Thus, the required probability is $\frac{1}{2} : 1 = \frac{1}{2}$.

Method 3 (see Figure 6):

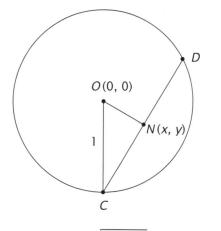

$$ON = \sqrt{x^2 + y^2} \text{ and } CD = 2\sqrt{1 - (x^2 + y^2)}.$$

Figure 6

Therefore,

$$CD \geq \sqrt{3}$$

$$\Leftrightarrow \quad 2\sqrt{1 - (x^2 + y^2)} \geq \sqrt{3}$$

$$\Leftrightarrow \quad 4 - 4(x^2 + y^2) \geq 3$$

$$\Leftrightarrow \quad (x^2 + y^2) \leq \frac{1}{4}$$

$\Leftrightarrow \quad$ Point $N(x, y)$ lies inside the circle with center $O(0, 0)$ and with radius $\frac{1}{2}$.

Thus, the required probability is given by the ratio

$$\frac{\text{area of a circle centered at point } O \text{ with radius } \frac{1}{2}}{\text{area of a circle centered at point } O \text{ with radius } 1} = \frac{\frac{1}{4}\pi}{\pi} = \frac{1}{4}.$$

The three probabilities obtained are all different because the three random methods are different. A random *angle* is used in Method 1, and the probability is $\frac{1}{3}$. A random *distance* from point O is used in Method 2, and the probability is $\frac{1}{2}$. A random *point* is used in Method 3, and the probability is $\frac{1}{4}$.

The probability of an event that occurs at random depends on the method of randomization, which can be specified in several different ways.

Comments

- Just before presenting this task, it might be interesting to note that $\sqrt{3}$ is the length of the side of the equilateral triangle inscribed in a unit circle. Students should be able to verify this. Following this, it may appear more natural to study the probability of getting a chord of length $\sqrt{3}$ at random.

- No matter which method we choose, it would be reasonable to expect that the probability of selecting a chord with a predetermined length would be the same. The fact that the probability depends on the mechanism of randomly selecting the chord is therefore quite surprising. The proper use of the term *probability* requires the specification of a definite experiment. The term *at random* cannot be left unclear; if it is, different people may design different methods of randomization and thus may get different results, which is what happened in this activity.

47 The Tennis Ball Paradox

Francisco and Eve play a rather unusual tennis game. They have an infinite sequence of tennis balls labeled 1, 2, 3, . . . and a very large box. Eve hops into the box. Francisco hits the tennis balls into the box and Eve hits them out, according to the following rules:

At time $t = 0$ they play Game 1. Francisco hits balls 1 and 2 into the box, and Eve immediately hits ball 1 out.

At time $t = \frac{1}{2}$ they play Game 2. Francisco hits balls 3 and 4 into the box, and Eve hits ball 2 out.

At time $t = \frac{3}{4}$ they play Game 3. Francisco hits balls 5 and 6 into the box, and Eve hits ball 3 out.

They continue in this way. Game n is played at time $t = 1 - \left(\frac{1}{2}\right)^{n-1}$, so t gets closer and closer to 1 and the tennis balls are being hit in and out faster and furiouser. At time $t = 1$, it is all over and Francisco and Eve can relax, having played an infinite number of games.

Take a look inside the box. Do you expect to find any tennis balls in it?

Francisco's reaction to this question is, "There must surely be an infinite number of tennis balls in the box. In each game I hit two balls into the box and Eve hit one out, giving a net gain of one ball in the box. Thus, after game n I would expect to find n balls in the box. I would therefore expect the number of balls in the box to increase to infinity."

Eve disagrees, saying, "At the end of the game the box is empty. Fix your attention on any particular ball, labeled k. Because I hit it out of the box in game k, it is not in the box. Therefore, there are no balls in the box."

What do you say? Can you resolve Francisco and Eve's disagreement?

47

The Tennis Ball Paradox

Explanation

Eve's argument is decisive. Because every tennis ball that Francisco hit into the box was eventually hit out of the box by Eve, no tennis ball remains. At any time before $t = 1$ there are tennis balls in the box, but at $t = 1$ there are none.

The infinite process described in this activity is impossible to carry out in the finite, physical world. In the real world, everything is finite. Hence, there is no real model for infinity—it is entirely a construct of the human mind. Consequently, the concept of infinity often leads to conflicts between our intuition, which is based on real-world experience, and the abstract notion of infinity.

See Also

See also Activities 48 and 49.

48 Center of Gravity Paradox

1. Do you know where the center of gravity of a rod lies? And the center of gravity of a triangle?

2. Suppose we allow side *BC* of triangle *ABC* to become shorter while allowing the altitude of the triangle to remain the same. What happens to the center of gravity of the triangle?

3. If we go to the limit, the triangle degenerates into a straight line. The centers of gravity of the triangles remain at the same height (one-third of the way above the base), but the center of gravity of the straight line (the degenerated triangle) is halfway up that line. It looks as if at some stage the center of gravity jumps from one-third of the way from the base to halfway up. How is this possible?

KEY CONCEPTS
- Continuity and discontinuity
- Limits
- Midpoints
- Point of intersection of medians

48

Center of Gravity Paradox

Explanation

1. The center of gravity of a uniform rod is at the midpoint of the rod. The center of gravity of a triangle is at the point of intersection of the three medians of the triangles. It is one-third of the way up each median (see Figure 1).

2. As side *BC* gets shorter, point *A* remains at the same height above side *BC*. Because point *G* is a point two-thirds of the way down the median from point *A* to side *BC,* the center of gravity of the triangle is also moving parallel to side *BC.*

3. The center of gravity shows a discontinuity in its behavior. Although the triangle changes continuously and in the limit "becomes" a straight line, the center of gravity of the limit is not the same as the limit of the centers of gravity of the triangles.

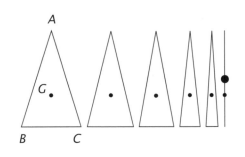

Figure 1

Comments

- The triangle, a two-dimensional object, in some sense "becomes" a straight line, a one-dimensional object. We expect continuous behavior in limiting situations such as this, but this is simply a situation in which continuity fails.

- A similar paradox results from collapsing a tetrahedron to a triangle of the same height. The center of gravity of a tetrahedron of height *h* is at a distance of $\frac{h}{4}$ above its base, while the center of gravity of a triangle of height *h* is $\frac{h}{3}$ above its base.

See Also

See also Activities 47 and 49.

One Equals Zero and Other Mathematical Surprises ©1998 by Key Curriculum Press

49 The Paradox of the Locked Boxes

Imagine an infinite row of boxes, each unlocked, each with a key in its lock.

At time $t = \frac{1}{2}$, lock Box 1 and put its key into Box 2.

At time $t = \frac{3}{4}$, lock Box 2 and put its key into Box 3.

> .
> .
> .

At time $t = 1 - \frac{1}{2^n}$, lock Box n and put its key into Box $n + 1$.

At time $t = 1$, all the boxes are locked and there are no keys in sight. So the boxes cannot be unlocked!

Can you explain this?

49

The Paradox of the Locked Boxes

Explanation

Any *finite* number of boxes locked in this way could be unlocked. The idea of locking an *infinite* number of boxes in this way is purely imaginary. Thus, it is not surprising when our expectations that the properties of finite situations will carry over to imaginary infinite situations are not realized.

Comments

- Students can be expected to provide this explanation: It is impossible to describe how the boxes can be unlocked because the process itself is a never-ending one. To unlock the boxes, we would have to get to the last box. But the process is infinite and there is no such "last box," so there is no box with which to start the unlocking process. (See also Activity 50.)

- Danish mathematician and humorist Piet Hein wrote:

  > A bit beyond perception's reach
  > I sometimes believe I see
  > That Life is two locked boxes, each
  > Containing the other's key.[19]

See Also

See also Activities 47, 48, 50, and 51.

---

[19] Piet Hein, *Still More Grooks* (London: Hodder Paperbacks, 1970): 47.

50 The Running Dog

Two children take their dog for a walk. Starting at the same point, the children walk away from each other in opposite directions, each walking at 2 meters per second. The dog runs to one child, then immediately turns and runs to the other, turns around and runs back to the first child, and so on.

The dog runs at 10 meters per second. After 10 seconds, the dog has run 100 meters and the children are 40 meters apart.

Where is the dog relative to the two children?

50

The Running Dog

Explanation

The question cannot be answered because the conditions of the problem cannot be met.

At the moment when the two children and the dog set off from the same point, the dog runs faster than the children, so immediately ceases to be between them. To be able to run from one to the other, the dog must pause for a moment to let the children move apart. The length of that short pause will determine where the dog is after 10 seconds.

Comments

- Think of the situation in reverse.

  Suppose the two children are 40 meters apart and the dog is somewhere between them. The children walk at 2 meters per second toward each other, and the dog runs back and forth between them at 10 meters per second.

  After 10 seconds the children meet, and the dog is between them. Wherever she started, the dog has run 100 meters. If we know only that the three come together after 10 seconds, there is no way of knowing where the dog was at the start.

- The process of the two children and the dog coming together is an example of an infinite procedure that cannot be reversed *because* it is infinite. (See also Activity 49.)[20]

See Also

See also Activities 47, 48, 49, and 51.

---

[20] For further reading, see Eli Maor, *To Infinity and Beyond: A Cultural History of the Infinite* (Boston: Birkhauser Boston, 1987).

51 The Explorer Paradox

An explorer lands on the Antarctic continent and sets out in a steady southeasterly direction. His map is a Mercator projection, which is a correspondence between points of the (x, y)-plane and points on the surface of the sphere. At the bottom of the map is the South Pole. On the map the explorer's route is a straight line (see Figure 1).

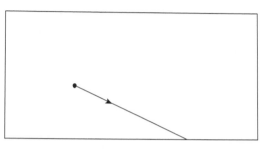

Figure 1

On the surface of the earth, which is a sphere, the explorer finds that the South Pole is always on his right. His route spirals around the pole in ever-decreasing circles, as shown in Figure 2. Eventually he reaches the South Pole.

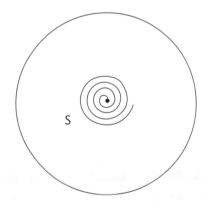

Figure 2

How can the explorer retrace his footsteps? He would have to walk in a northwesterly direction, but when he is at the South Pole every direction is north!

51

The Explorer Paradox

Explanation

The explorer cannot retrace his footsteps. This is an example of an infinite process that cannot be reversed. Such a process exists only in the mind. In the physical world only finite processes are realizable. As the explorer approaches the South Pole, he is always facing southeast. In the limit, he is facing north!

See Also

See also Activities 47, 48, 49, and 50.

52 A Surprise Limit

In Figure 1 below, *OBQ* is a semicircle of radius 1, with point *O* at the origin and point *Q* on the *x*-axis. *OB* is a chord, and point *A* is on the *y*-axis, with *OB* = *OA* = *h* < 2. Join points *A* and *B* to form segment *AB* and extend this segment to intersect the *x*-axis at point *P*. What happens as *h* tends to 0? It seems reasonably clear that the line *ABP* gets closer and closer to the *x*-axis and that point *P* moves to the right. Does the length of segment *OP* tend to infinity as *h* tends to 0, or does it tend to a finite limit?

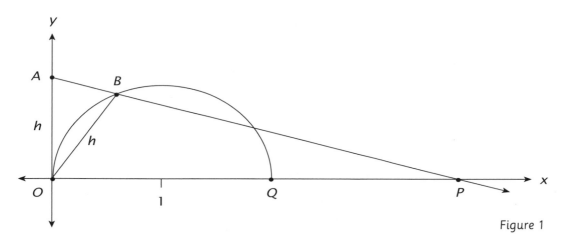

Figure 1

Explore these questions by experimenting with a ruler and a compass or with a geometry computer program such as The Geometer's Sketchpad®. (For small values of *h*, accurate constructions are very difficult.) Note that you cannot just let *h* = 0, because then the point *P* is not well defined. You have to let *h* *tend to* 0 without ever getting there.

What would your guess for $\lim_{h\to0} OP$ be? Could $\lim_{h\to0} OP = 4$ be true?

52

A Surprise Limit

Explanation

Point P indeed tends to $(4, 0)$.

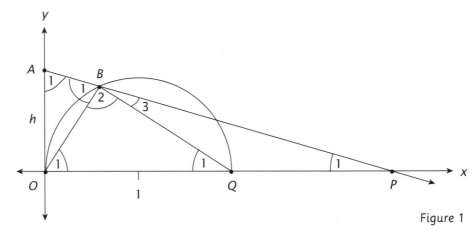

Figure 1

Proof:

Join points B and Q to form segment BQ. Then look at the angles in the figure.

$\angle B_2 = 90°$ (The angle in a semicircle.)

$\angle A_1 = 90° - \angle P_1$ ($\triangle AOP$ is a right-angled triangle.)

$\angle B_1 = 90° - \angle B_3.$

Because $\angle B_1 = \angle A_1$ ($\triangle AOB$ is isosceles), we deduce that $\angle P_1 = \angle B_3$, and it follows that $BQ = QP$.

Now, as h tends to 0, point B tends to point O; thus $BQ \to OQ$ as $h \to 0$.

Thus, $OP = OQ + QP = OQ + BQ \to 2OQ = 4$ as $h \to 0$.

Comments

- Most will guess that point P tends to infinity as h tends to 0.

- This solution can be worked out by coordinate geometry as well by expressing line OP in terms of h.

See Also

See also Activity 60.[21]

---

[21] For further reading, see W. A. Leonard and H. S. Schultz, "Two Surprising Limits," *Mathematical Gazette* 66, no. 437 (October 1982).

We obtain the solution formula $x = \frac{-b \pm \sqrt{b^2 - 4ac}}{2a}$ of the quadratic equation $ax^2 + b + x + c = 0$ under the assumption that $a \neq 0$, so we cannot let $a = 0$. However, we could let a tend to 0. Assuming that $b \neq 0$ as we let a tend to 0, we would expect to get as a solution $\frac{c}{b}$, the solution of the linear equation $bx + c = 0$. However, invoking L'Hospital's rule, we get two solutions:

$$\lim_{a \to 0} \frac{-b \pm \sqrt{b^2 - 4ac}}{2a} = \lim_{a \to 0} \frac{\pm \frac{-4c}{2\sqrt{b^2 - 4ac}}}{2} = \lim_{a \to 0} \pm \frac{c}{\sqrt{b^2 - 4ac}} = \pm \frac{c}{|b|}.$$

Why did we get two solutions?

53

The Quadratic Formula Revisited

Explanation

To invoke L'Hospital's rule, a "0/0" situation is required. In the quadratic formula, the limit of the denominator as $a \to 0$ is certainly 0. Look what happens to the numerator as a tends to 0: $\lim_{a \to 0} - b \pm \sqrt{b^2 - 4ac} = -b \pm \sqrt{b^2} = 0$ if $b > 0$ and we use the positive sign, or if $b < 0$ and we use the negative sign. Only in these cases can we use L'Hospital's rule, and then in each case the rule gives the limit as $-\frac{c}{b}$, as expected.

Comments

- This activity starts with a reminder that the quadratic formula is obtained under the assumption that $a \neq 0$ and that therefore $a = 0$ cannot be used (see also Activity 14). Using zero when a nonzero assumption has been made is sometimes very difficult to resist. For example, the definition of the derivative as the limit of a Newton quotient $\frac{f(a + h) - f(a)}{h}$ yields the following for $f(x) = x^2$:

$$\frac{(x + h)^2 - x^2}{h} = 2x + h.$$

  The temptation now is to let $h = 0$ and get $2x$. But because we just obtained $2x + h$ by canceling h, that is, by assuming that $h \neq 0$, we cannot let $h = 0$. However, it is all right to let h *tend to* 0.

- Another assumption in this activity is that $b \neq 0$. What happens if $b = 0$? Students should be able to answer this question themselves.

- This activity is a reminder that whenever a theorem is applied, we must check that the assumptions on which the theorem is based are true. If not, we might obtain the wrong results.

Historical Background

L'Hospital's rule was published in the first textbook on calculus, entitled *Analyse des infiniment petits* (1696) and written by French nobleman and amateur mathematician Marquis de L'Hospital (1661–1704). In 1691, he hired Johann Bernoulli (1667–1748) to teach him calculus, then a revolutionary and new subject. L'Hospital bought Bernoulli's rights to his mathematical findings, collected Bernoulli's writings, and wrote the book. The rule itself was communicated to L'Hospital by Johann Bernoulli in a letter.[22]

---

[22] For more details, see D. J. Struik, *Mathematics Teacher* 56 (1963): 257–266.

54 A Stairway to Paradox

Consider the infinite stairway $x^{x^{x^{\cdot^{\cdot^{\cdot}}}}}$. Let's assume that $x > 0$ and that x^{x^x} means $x^{(x^x)}$, that $x^{x^{x^x}}$ means $x^{(x^{x^x})}$, and so on. In the equation $x^{x^{x^{\cdot^{\cdot^{\cdot}}}}} = 2$, the exponent of the x at the bottom of the stairway is just $x^{x^{x^{\cdot^{\cdot^{\cdot}}}}}$, which is equal to 2. Thus, the equation becomes $x^2 = 2$ and the solution (because $x > 0$) is $x = \sqrt{2}$.

Now consider a second equation, $x^{x^{x^{\cdot^{\cdot^{\cdot}}}}} = 4$. Reasoning as we just did, the equation can be written $x^4 = 4$ and again the solution is $x = \sqrt{2}$.

Because $\sqrt{2}$ satisfies the first equation, $\sqrt{2}^{\sqrt{2}^{\sqrt{2}^{\cdot^{\cdot^{\cdot}}}}} = 2$. Because $\sqrt{2}$ satisfies the second equation, $\sqrt{2}^{\sqrt{2}^{\sqrt{2}^{\cdot^{\cdot^{\cdot}}}}} = 4$. So we have proved that 2 = 4.

What led to this paradox?

KEY CONCEPTS
- Equations
- Exponents
- Operations, order of
- Solution, existence of
- Square roots

54

A Stairway to Paradox

Explanation

Evaluating the sequence $\sqrt{2}$, $\sqrt{2}^{\sqrt{2}}$, $\sqrt{2}^{\sqrt{2}^{\sqrt{2}}}$, ... on a calculator gives

1.4142136

1.6325269

1.7608396

1.8409109

.

.

.

The numbers seem to increase steadily toward 2 but never exceed 2.

This can be carefully proved. Suppose $a_1 = \sqrt{2}$, $a_2 = \sqrt{2}^{\sqrt{2}}$, $a_3 = \sqrt{2}^{\sqrt{2}^{\sqrt{2}}}$, and in general $a_{(n+1)} = \left(\sqrt{2}\right)^{a_n}$. Now we certainly know that $a_1 < 2$. Further, if $a_n < 2$, then

$$a_{(n+1)} = \left(\sqrt{2}\right)^{a_n} < \left(\sqrt{2}\right)^2 = 2.$$

Thus, by mathematical induction, $a_n < 2$ for all $n \geq 1$.

We also know that $a_2 > a_1$. Further, if $a_{(n+1)} > a_n$, then

$$\frac{a_{(n+2)}}{a_{(n+1)}} = \frac{\left(\sqrt{2}\right)^{a_{(n+1)}}}{\left(\sqrt{2}\right)^{a_n}} = \sqrt{2}^{(a_{(n+1)} - a_n)} > 1,$$

so $a_{(n+2)} > a_{(n+1)}$.

Once again, mathematical induction shows that $a_{(n+1)} > a_n$ for all $n \geq 1$.

Therefore, $\{a_n\}$ is an increasing sequence of real numbers that is bounded above. Such a sequence converges. Let's denote its limit by a: $a_n \to a$. Because the exponential function $y = \left(\sqrt{2}\right)^x$ is continuous, it follows that as $a_n \to a$, so $\left(\sqrt{2}\right)^{a_n} \to \left(\sqrt{2}\right)^a$. But $\left(\sqrt{2}\right)^{a_n} = a_{(n+1)}$, which also converges to a. Hence, $\left(\sqrt{2}\right)^a = a$.

By considering the graphs of $y = \left(\sqrt{2}\right)^x$ and $y = x$, we can easily see that $\left(\sqrt{2}\right)^x = x$ has just two solutions: $x = 2$ and $x = 4$ (see Figure 1).

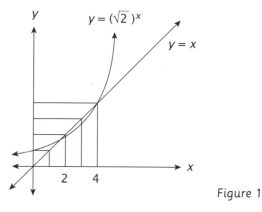

Figure 1

Now, $a \neq 4$ (because $a_n \leq 2$ and $a_n \to a$, $a \leq 2$), so $a = 2$. This completes the proof that $\sqrt{2}^{\sqrt{2}^{\sqrt{2}^{\cdots}}} = 2$.

Now let us return to $x^{x^{x^{\cdots}}} = 4$, which in the activity results in the solution $x = \sqrt{2}$. The error that led to this paradox occurred in our very first step, when we assumed that the equation *had* a solution. Our assumption led us to the "solution" $\sqrt{2}$. Actually we found that the only possible candidate for a solution is $\sqrt{2}$, if the equation has one. We have just shown that $\sqrt{2}$ does *not* satisfy the equation $\sqrt{2}^{\sqrt{2}^{\sqrt{2}^{\cdots}}} = 4$ because $\sqrt{2}^{\sqrt{2}^{\sqrt{2}^{\cdots}}} \neq 4$; therefore, we must conclude that the equation has no solution.

Comments

- The paradox in this activity rests on solving two equations. Its intriguing feature is that one of the solutions is correct and the other is wrong. When your students have studied the solutions of the two equations, but before going any further, you might tell them that one solution method is correct, the other wrong, and invite them to decide which is correct.

- This paradox illustrates very well how introducing a false assumption into a line of reasoning can lead to a contradiction. Here the assumption appears to be innocuous: we assume the given equation has a solution. The consequent contradiction is very subtle because our false assumption that a solution exists apparently enables us to find it. (For a similar situation, see Activity 23.)

- This problem is commonly attributed to Swiss mathematician Leonhard Euler (1707–1783).[23]

---

[23] For further reading, see "FFF #60: A Two-Valued Function," *The College Mathematics Journal* 24, no. 3 (May 1993): 230.

---

55 A Calculus Proof That 1 = 2

We know that $2 + 2 = 2^2$, $3 + 3 + 3 = 3^2$, $4 + 4 + 4 + 4 = 4^2$, and so on.

In general, $x + x + \ldots + x = x^2$, where there are x number of xs on the left-hand side of the equation.

Now, differentiate both sides:

$$1 + 1 + \ldots + 1 = 2x.$$

Because there are x number of 1s on the left-hand side of the equation, we deduce that

$$x = 2x$$

and it follows that

$$1 = 2.$$

Where is the flaw in this reasoning?

One Equals Zero and Other Mathematical Surprises ©1998 by Key Curriculum Press

55

A Calculus Proof That $1 = 2$

Explanation

There are two major flaws in the reasoning. The first relates to the equation

$$x + x + \ldots + x = x^2 \quad \text{(with } x \text{ terms on the left).}$$

This equality is certainly true if x is a positive integer, but the left-hand side of the equation is meaningless if x is negative, a fraction, or an irrational number. Now, to differentiate a function at a point, the function must be defined not just at that point but on a neighborhood of the point—an open interval containing the point. Because the left-hand side is defined only if x is a positive integer, it cannot be differentiated.

Even if this obstacle could be removed, there is a flaw in the process of differentiation. The rule used is that the derivative of a sum is the sum of the derivatives. This rule applies if the number of terms is fixed, not variable. Because the number of terms is itself a variable in our case, we have no right to expect the rule to apply.

Comment

The error made in this activity is analogous to that commonly made by beginning calculus students who apply the rule $\frac{d}{dx}(x^n) = nx^{(n-1)}$, where n is fixed, in an attempt to differentiate a^x: $\frac{d}{dx}(a^x) = xa^{(x-1)}$.

See Also

See also Activities 53, 56, 57, and 60.

56 Two Wrongs Make a Right

A teacher asked his class to differentiate x^x.

Keiko used the rule $\frac{d}{dx}(x^n) = nx^{(n-1)}$ and obtained the answer $\frac{d}{dx}(x^x) = x \cdot x^{(x-1)} = x^x$. Barbara used the rule $\frac{d}{dx}(a^x) = a^x \cdot \ln a$ and obtained the answer $\frac{d}{dx}(x^x) = x^x \cdot \ln x$.

Nikolai did not know how to do the problem, so he just added Keiko's answer to Barbara's answer, obtaining $\frac{d}{dx}(x^x) = x^x + x^x \cdot \ln x = x^x(1 + \ln x)$.

The teacher told Keiko and Barbara that their answers were wrong but that Nikolai's was right!

Can you explain why?

Nice work, Nikolai!!

56

Two Wrongs Make a Right

Explanation

The rule Keiko used, $\frac{d}{dx}(x^n) = nx^{(n-1)}$, requires n to be a constant. Similarly, Barbara's rule, $\frac{d}{dx}(a^x) = a^x \cdot \ln a$, requires a to be constant. Neither rule can be applied to differentiate x^x, where neither the base nor the exponent is constant.

The method the teacher expected his students to use is one known as logarithmic differentiation: we first take logs of both sides and then we differentiate.

Here we have the function $y = x^x$.

Take logs:

$$\ln y = x \ln x.$$

Differentiate:

$$\frac{1}{y} \cdot \frac{dy}{dx} = x \cdot \frac{1}{x} + \ln x = 1 + \ln x$$

$$\Rightarrow \qquad \frac{dy}{dx} = y(1 + \ln x) = x^x(1 + \ln x).$$

Comment

Is it just a lucky chance that Nikolai's answer, obtained by adding two wrong answers, gives the right result? Surprisingly not! The reason lies in the chain rule for differentiating a function of two variables.

If $y = u^v$ such that u and v are both functions of x, the chain rule gives

$$\frac{dy}{dx} = \frac{\partial y}{\partial u} \cdot \frac{du}{dx} + \frac{\partial y}{\partial v} \cdot \frac{dv}{dx}$$

$$= vu^{(v-1)} \cdot \frac{du}{dx} + u^v \cdot \ln u \cdot \frac{dv}{dx}.$$

Now, if $u(x) = v(x) = x$, then $\frac{du}{dx} = \frac{dv}{dx} = 1$ and

$$\frac{dy}{dx} = x \cdot x^{(x-1)} \cdot 1 + x^x \cdot \ln x \cdot 1 = x^x \cdot (1 + \ln x),$$

which is the sum of the two wrong answers.

See Also

See also Activities 53, 55, 57, and 60. For another lucky mistake, see Activity 4.

---

57 Area, Surface, and Volume

The area of a circle of radius r is πr^2.
The circumference of a circle of radius r is $2\pi r$.
The derivative of πr^2 is $2\pi r$.
Thus the derivative of the area is the circumference.

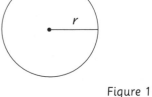

Figure 1

The volume of a sphere of radius r is $\frac{4}{3}\pi r^3$.
The surface area of a sphere of radius r is $4\pi r^2$.
The derivative of $\frac{4}{3}\pi r^3$ is $4\pi r^2$.
Thus the derivative of the volume is the surface area.

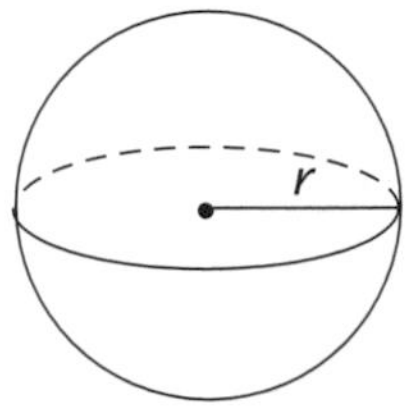

Are these results just coincidences?

Try the same idea with squares and cubes.

Figure 2

The area of a square with side length a is a^2.
The perimeter of a square with side length a is $4a$.
The derivative of a^2 is $2a$, which is *not* the perimeter.

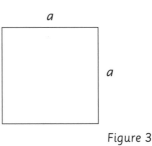

Figure 3

The volume of a cube with side length a is a^3.
The surface area of a cube with side length a is $6a^2$.
The derivative of a^3 is $3a^2$, which is not the surface area.

Maybe the results of the first two cases (the circle and the sphere) were indeed just coincidences.

What do you think?

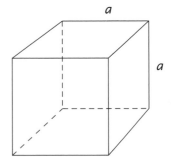

Figure 4

KEY CONCEPTS
- Area
- Circumference
- Derivatives
- Surface area and volume of solids

57

Area, Surface, and Volume

Explanation

The results of the first two cases are *not* coincidences.

Consider the case of the circle. When we differentiate the expression for the area, we are calculating the limit, as h tends to 0, of the Newton quotient $\frac{\pi(r + h)^2 - \pi r^2}{h}$.

Now, the top line of this area expression, in geometric terms, is the area of the strip shown in Figure 5.

This strip has width h and inside length $2\pi r$. Thus,
$$\frac{\pi(r + h)^2 - \pi r^2}{h} \approx \frac{2\pi rh}{h} = 2\pi r.$$

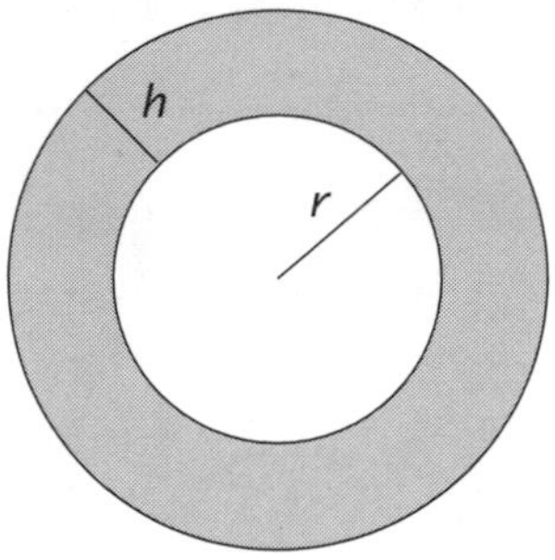

Figure 5

Therefore, it is not at all surprising that the derivative of the formula for the area of a circle gives the circumference.

A similar argument holds for the sphere. When differentiating the formula for the volume of a sphere, we are calculating the limit as h tends to 0 of the Newton quotient

$$\frac{\frac{4}{3}\pi(r + h)^3 - \frac{4}{3}\pi r^3}{h}.$$

Now the top line of this volume expression, in geometric terms, is the volume of a spherical shell of thickness h and inside area $4\pi r^2$. Therefore,

$$\frac{\frac{4}{3}\pi(r + h)^3 - \frac{4}{3}\pi r^3}{h} \approx \frac{4\pi r^2 h}{h} = 4\pi r^2$$

and we see that it is no coincidence that the derivative of the volume of a circle is its surface area.

Why, then, does this not work for the square or the cube? The fact is that it does if we measure the square and the cube from their centers, as we did for the circle and the sphere.

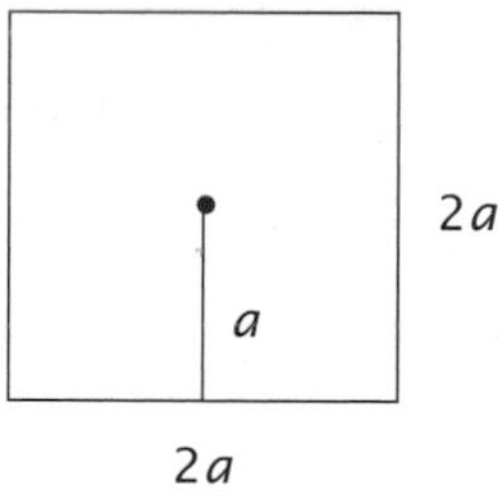

In Figure 6, the square has side length $2a$, area $4a^2$, and circumference $8a$, which is the derivative of its area. This is just what you would expect from the Newton quotient for $4a^2$,

$$\frac{4(a + h)^2 - 4a^2}{h}.$$

Figure 6

The numerator is represented geometrically by four strips of length $2a$ and width h, plus four little squares of side h, as shown in Figure 7. The total area is $8ah + 4h^2$. Dividing by h gives $8a + 4h$, which, as h tends to 0, tends to $8a$, the circumference of the square.

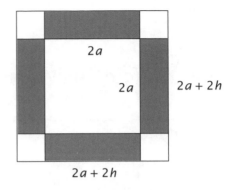

A similar argument applies to the cube. The Newton quotient for the volume is

$$\frac{8(a + h)^3 - 8a^3}{h}.$$

Figure 7

The numerator, in geometric terms, is the volume of the outer layer of width h of a cube with side length $2a$ (see Figure 8), namely, six square face tiles of side length $2a$ and thickness h (volume $4a^2h$), twelve prisms with square cross sections of length $2a$ and side length h, and eight small cubes of side length h. Thus, the total volume of the outer layer is $6 \cdot 4a^2h + 12 \cdot 2ah^2 + 8h^3$.

Dividing by h gives $24a^2 + 24ah + 8h^2$, which, as h tends to 0, tends to $24a^2$, the surface area of the cube.

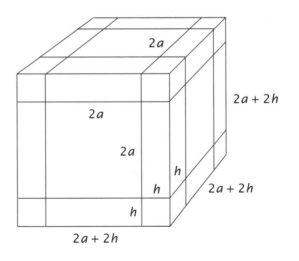

Figure 8

See Also

For related activities, see also Activities 36 and 58.

58 The Alpenhorn Paradox

Once upon a time there was a Swiss mathematician who loved playing the alpenhorn. One day she decided to design her own. She took the curve $y = \frac{1}{x}$ ($x \geq 1$) and rotated it about the x-axis (see Figure 1).

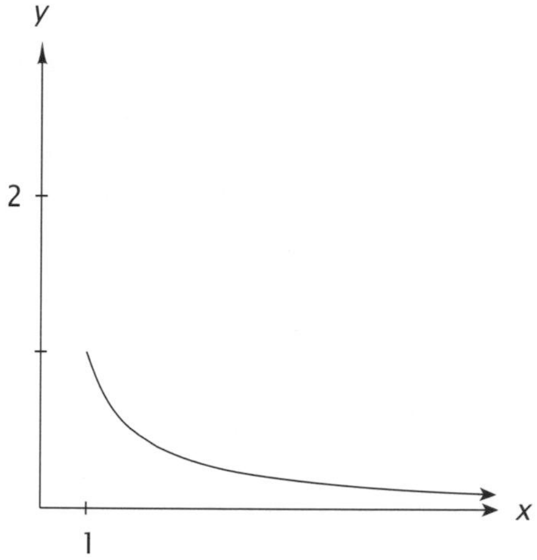

She decided to paint the inside of the alpenhorn with bright colors. Being a mathematician, she knew how to calculate the surface area of her alpenhorn because she knew that the formula for calculating the area of the surface, obtained by rotating a curve $y = f(x)$ ($a \leq x \leq b$) about the x-axis, is

Figure 1

$$\text{Surface area} = 2\pi \int_a^b f(x)\sqrt{1 + [f'(x)]^2}\,dx.$$

Letting $f(x) = \frac{1}{x}$, $a = 1$, and $b = \infty$, she obtained

$$2\pi \int_1^\infty \frac{1}{x}\sqrt{1 + \left(-\frac{1}{x^2}\right)^2}\,dx = 2\pi \int_1^\infty \frac{\sqrt{x^4 + 1}}{x^3}\,dx.$$

She was not able to evaluate this integral in the usual way by finding an indefinite integral. However, she noticed that

$$2\pi \int_1^\infty \frac{1}{x^3}\sqrt{1 + x^4}\,dx \geq 2\pi \int_1^\infty \frac{1}{x^3}\sqrt{x^4}\,dx = 2\pi \int_1^\infty \frac{1}{x}\,dx = 2\pi \ln x\,|_1^\infty = \infty.$$

Thus, she realized that her alpenhorn had infinite surface area and would presumably need an infinite amount of paint.

Having calculated the surface area of her alpenhorn, she wondered about its volume. She knew that the formula for the volume of a solid of revolution, obtained by rotating a curve $y = f(x)$ ($a \leq x \leq b$) about the x-axis, is

$$\text{Volume} = \pi \int_a^b [f(x)]^2\,dx.$$

Letting $f(x) = \frac{1}{x}$, $a = 1$, and $b = \infty$, she obtained $\pi \int_1^\infty \frac{1}{x^2}\,dx = \pi\left(-\frac{1}{x}\right)\Big|_1^\infty = \pi.$

She therefore ordered π units of paint, poured it into her alpenhorn and poured it out again. She not only painted the infinite surface area of her alpenhorn, but she also had some paint left over!

Is that really possible?

KEY CONCEPTS
- Finite integrals
- Infinity
- Solids of revolution
- Surface area and volume of solids

58

The Alpenhorn Paradox

Explanation

The calculations are correct: the alpenhorn has finite volume but infinite surface area. When we paint something, the layer of paint has a uniform positive thickness, so an infinite surface area would certainly need an infinite amount of paint. This is what our mathematician would find if she tried to paint the *outside* of her alpenhorn. But the *inside* of the alpenhorn cannot be painted with a uniformly thick coat of paint because the alpenhorn gets narrower and narrower.

Comments

- In this activity we have an example of a solid with infinite surface area yet with finite volume.

  To complete the discussion of this activity with a smile, you might raise the question, What happens where the radius of the alpenhorn is less than the thickness of the coat of paint? In practical terms, of course, a coat of paint, however thin, does not have zero thickness. So, when the radius of the alpenhorn is less than the thickness of the coat of paint, the paint will block the alpenhorn completely, making it impossible to blow!

- From the mathematical point of view it is no surprise that a solid exists that has infinite surface area and finite volume. Consider the reverse problem: Does a solid exist that has finite surface area and infinite volume? The answer is certainly not, because among all solids of a given (finite) surface area, the sphere has the maximum volume.

- This paradox brings up (as do several others in this book) the notion of infinity, which is the unique creation of mathematics. Infinity does not exist in the physical world. It only exists in the human mind or imagination, where all of mathematics is developed. Nevertheless, infinity is a very useful notion in the sciences, and its application to the physical world is of great importance.

- The alpenhorn is a solid of finite volume generated by rotating a region of infinite area. (The area of the region rotated is $\int_1^\infty \frac{1}{x}dx = \ln x \,|_1^\infty = \infty$.)

  Another paradox, converse to this activity in a way, has been observed by John Dawson,[24] who presents a solid of revolution having an infinite volume but generated by a region of finite area.

---

[24] John W. Dawson, "Contrasting Examples in Improper Integration," *Mathematics Teacher* 84 (March 1990): 201–202.

Consider the function

$$f(x) = \begin{cases} 1 & 0 \le x \le 1 \\ \dfrac{1}{x^2} & 1 \le x \le \infty \end{cases}.$$

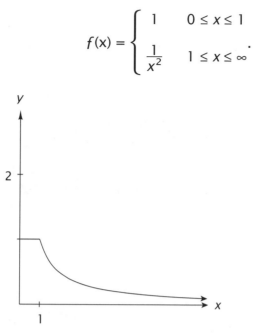

Figure 2

The area under the curve shown in Figure 2 is $1 + \displaystyle\int_1^\infty \frac{1}{x^2}dx = 1 + \left(-\frac{1}{x}\right)\Big|_1^\infty = 2.$

Now rotate the region about the y-axis to get the solid of revolution that Dawson calls Thor's anvil, shown in Figure 3.

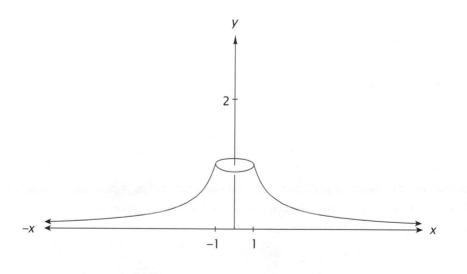

Figure 3

This solid has volume $\pi \displaystyle\int_0^1 x^2 dy = \pi \int_0^1 \frac{1}{y}dy = \pi \ln y\big|_0^1 = \infty.$

See Also

For related activities, see also Activities 36 and 57.

---

59 The Surprise Test Paradox

1. On Friday afternoon a teacher announces to her class, "There will be a test one day next week, but the day will be a complete surprise."

   After giving the matter a little thought, Anne reasons that the test cannot be left until Friday because if it has not taken place on Thursday, everybody will know for sure that it has to take place on Friday. Thus, it will not be a complete surprise.

   But then, says Tashi, the test cannot take place on Thursday: if it has not taken place by Wednesday afternoon, everybody will know it has to take place on Thursday because Anne has shown it will not take place on Friday. Hence, Thursday is out, too, because otherwise how could the test be a complete surprise?

   Using the same reasoning, Caroline deduces that the test cannot take place on Wednesday and Deon immediately notices that it cannot take place on Tuesday. Hui then clinches the paradox with the observation that the test cannot take place on Monday.

   Triumphantly the students present their reasoning to their teacher. Can you explain this paradox?

2. Can the teacher get around the paradox somehow and still surprise her students with a test?

One Equals Zero and Other Mathematical Surprises ©1998 by Key Curriculum Press

59

The Surprise Test Paradox

Explanation

1. This is a little like the Frank Sinatra song about an irresistible force meeting an immovable object. Something's gotta give.

   The teacher has in fact made two statements that cannot coexist. The first is that the test is certain to take place on one of the five days of the following week. So the probability that the test will take place during the week is 1. The second statement is that the occurrence of the test on any particular day will be a complete surprise. This can only mean that the probability it will take place on any particular day is zero.

   Suppose that the probabilities that the test will take place on Monday, Tuesday, Wednesday, Thursday, or Friday are p_1, p_2, p_3, p_4, and p_5, respectively. Because the test is certain to take place during the week, the probabilities add up to 1. But if $p_1 + p_2 + p_3 + p_4 + p_5 = 1$, the probabilities p_i cannot all be zero. If the probability that the test will take place on a certain day is positive, then the occurrence of the test on that day cannot be a complete surprise. The paradox consists in the teacher's postulating a finite probability space in which every event has zero probability.

2. When the teacher realized her mistake, she changed her mind and said, "There will be a one-hour test some time later today. The exact time that the test will commence will be a complete surprise."

   Because school ended at 4 p.m., everybody knew that the test had to commence at or before 3 p.m. But there was no way of reasoning backwards from that point in time. The test could commence at any of an infinite number of times during the day, with each moment in time up to 3 p.m. equally likely, with zero probability.

   So the paradox is resolved by acknowledging the possibility of an infinite number of zero probabilities adding up to 1, a certainty. That in itself is a paradox!

60 A Surprise Limit Revisited

In Figure 1, *OBQ* is a semicircle of radius 1, with point *O* at the origin and point *Q* on the *x*-axis. Let *A* be a point on the *y*-axis such that *OA* = *h* < 2, and let *B* be a point on the semicircle such that the length of arc *OB* is *h*. Join points *A* and *B* to form segment *AB* and extend it to intersect the *x*-axis at point *R*. What happens to point *R* as *h* tends to 0?

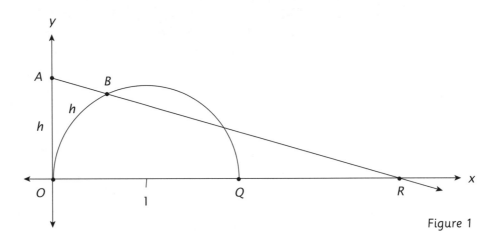

Figure 1

60

A Surprise Limit Revisited

KEY CONCEPTS
- Derivatives
- Functions, trigonometric
- Geometry
- L'Hospital's rule
- Limits

Explanation

In Figure 2 point A has coordinates $(0, h)$. Point B has coordinates $(1 - \cos h, \sin h)$. Segments AO and BT are corresponding sides of similar triangles AOR and BTR, so

$$\frac{OR}{h} = \frac{RT}{\sin h} = \frac{OR - OT}{\sin h} = \frac{OR - (1 - \cos h)}{\sin h}.$$

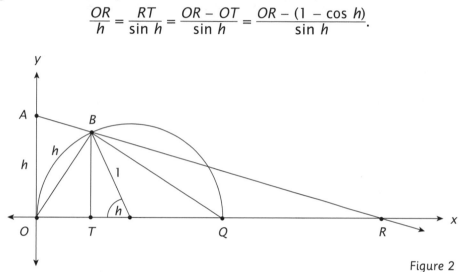

Figure 2

Solving for OR gives $OR = \dfrac{h(1 - \cos h)}{h - \sin h}$.

Determining the limit of this expression as h tends to 0 requires L'Hospital's rule:

$$\lim_{h \to 0} OR = \lim_{h \to 0} \frac{h(1 - \cos h)}{h - \sin h} \qquad \text{``}\frac{0}{0}\text{ form''}$$

$$= \lim_{h \to 0} \frac{1 - \cos h + h \sin h}{1 - \cos h} \qquad \text{``}\frac{0}{0}\text{'' again}$$

$$= \lim_{h \to 0} \frac{\sin h + \sin h + h \cos h}{\sin h}$$

$$= \left(2 + \lim_{h \to 0} \frac{h}{\sin h} \cdot \cos h \right)$$

$$= 3 \ \left(\text{because } \lim_{h \to 0} \frac{h}{\sin h} = 1 \text{ and } \lim_{h \to 0} \cos h = 1\right).$$

Comments

- If students have not solved the problem in Activity 52 before attacking this activity, many of them might be inclined to guess that the limit is infinity. If they have completed Activity 52, they should be able to see that $\lim_{h \to 0} OR \le 4$.

  Perhaps π would be a reasonable guess because $\pi < 4$ and the problem involves a circle. As proved in the explanation, this is not a good guess either.

- The calculation of $\lim_{h \to 0} OR$ requires the application of L'Hospital's rule twice. Most applications of this rule are confined to artificial textbook exercises. Here we have a real-world application for a change.

- For further reading, see Leonard and Schultz, and Webb.[25]

Historical Background

For more about the Marquis de L'Hospital and L'Hospital's rule, see also Activity 53.

---

[25] W. A. Leonard and H. S. Schultz, "Two Surprising Limits," *Mathematical Gazette* 66, no. 437 (October 1982): 223–224. J. H. Webb, "Two Surprising Limits Revisited," *Mathematical Gazette* 67, no. 442 (December 1983): 256–259.
